The Outer Hebrides

The Timeless Way

The Outer Hebrides

The Timeless Way

Peter Clarke

A walk through the Outer Hebridean islands of Scotland
www.outerhebridesway.org

Northampton Square Ltd
www.NorthamptonSq.com
2006

The Outer Hebrides
The Timeless Way
By
Peter Clarke

Text and maps copyright © Northampton Square Ltd 2006

First published in Great Britain in 2006 by
Northampton Square Ltd
26 Lewis Street
Stornoway
Isle of Lewis
HS1 2JF

www.NorthamptonSq.com

ISBN 0-9550696-0-2

British Library Cataloguing in Publication Data.
A catalogue record for this book is available on request from the British Library.

Typeset by Alistair Dabbs
Printed in Spain by GraphyCems

SAFETY

Be aware of the risks of taking the route suggested in this book especially when crossing the moors and tidal fords. Information is given in the Foreword and individual chapters about these crossings which may guide you across. If in doubt do not make the crossing. Always make sure someone is aware of your plans who can call help if you fail to arrive at your destination.

You walk this route through the islands at your own risk. Follow the Scottish Outdoor Access Code.
www.outdooraccess-scotland.com

CONTENTS

CONTENTS

LIST OF FIGURES

FOREWORD

THE AIM OF this book is to show how it is possible to walk through the islands using old tracks and ways. Over 50% of the route described is off road. The second aim is to start building a bridge of understanding with contemporary, southern, thinking about Scotland in general and the islands in particular.

I was born in Bedfordshire but first visited the islands in 1973. It was love at first sight. For most of the past thirty-odd years I have tried to explain this love to my southern friends. This book is part of that quest. Only after starting the book did I realise how far that bridge of understanding had to stretch. I hope that this book has at least built a foundation for that bridge.

The dilemma I faced was how best to explain the islands and convey the complex spirit of the place in its full glory. The islands are not a microcosm of society they are a discrete diverse society set within a vast wilderness. History and population movement have shrunk this society leaving many layers of history close to the surface.

My approach was to walk through the islands thus guaranteeing that the book started with the actual landscape of the islands, the things that could be seen by every visitor. But it quickly goes beyond the road, across the moors and over the horizon into the distant glens finding many forgotten places.

This book does not describe everything in the islands; it is no guide book. Nor is it a travelogue. It is based on my journey through the islands but it is not about that journey. Nor does it describe every aspect of Hebridean life or

ii

every incident in Hebridean history. Nor does it explore the beauty or the gaiety and poetry of the Gaelic. I am ashamed to confess that the wonderful Gaelic language is still inaccessible to me despite many attempts. I have attempted to explain why I love these islands and their people but I have probably failed most miserably in that task. But if I had not been in love I doubt if I would have struggled for so many years to publish this book.

At the end of the film *Blade Runner* the dying android looks up at the hero and says I have seen star ships ablaze on the edge of Orion. In one short phrase we see the richness of the android's life and the futility of ignoring, snuffing out, such rich experience. Over the years many of my friends have, I am sure, wondered if this exercise was futile. If this book achieves its goals, you will see the islands as a place of such profound beauty and grace that its existence cannot be ignored.

Thank you, dear reader, for your interest and faith. Let's us set forth on our journey. Together we can create an Outer Hebrides Way, not only a physical way but a way which secures the islands as a special place in our United Kingdom.

A safe journey.

Balemore, North Uist

MAPS, PLACE NAMES, SAFETY
AND OTHER NOTES

I HAVE PROVIDED sketch maps to help readers interpret the text. If you are planning to walk the Outer Hebrides Way it will be essential for you to purchase Sheets 9, 13, 14, 22 and 31 of the Ordnance Survey's 1:50,000 maps.

The text mentions over 570 places, townships, hills, lochs, burns and bays. I have had considerable trouble ensuring that I used a consistent and understandable form of name. Dwelly, in the foreword to his pioneering Gaelic dictionary, points to the difficulty of codifying Gaelic words. He found that Gaelic was primarily a spoken language and opinion varied on the written form of Gaelic words. Indeed opinion varied from place to place in respect of some words.

I decided to base the names I used in the text on the first edition of the 1:50,000 OS map. This edition uses largely Anglicised versions of place names which are still in popular usage. The local authority, then called Comhairle nan Eilean and now called Comhairle nan Eilean Siar, decided to use only the Gaelic versions of place names for road signs except in Stornoway and Benbecula where bilingual signs were to be adopted. They set about creating Gaelic versions of all place names. Some places had a Celtic origin, others a Viking origin. This policy is reflected in subsequent editions of the Ordnance Survey 1:50,000 maps.

Please use the maps provided to assist your navigation on the OS Maps. Cross reference the anglicised names with those on the maps and place names you will find along the way.

A note on place names by Petra Clarke

Place names in the Hebrides are usually descriptive of the physical features of the terrain or they may refer to crops or buildings. In many cases their derivation is Gaelic or old Norse. There are difficulties with spelling because local variations abound and the names of places, as recorded on atlases, continue to be modified up to today. There is often an anglicized version that has become so well used as to be permanent. In spite of these problems, it is an exciting exercise to puzzle out the meanings of place names. They often give an insight into former ways of life in the islands.

Some words are repeatedly incorporated into names. Beinn means mountain or high place, but most people are more familiar with the highest peak in Britain being called Ben Nevis. Abhainn means river; but this is so little known that tautology is excusable when referring to 'the River Abhainn …' Kin is the anglicised prefix of the Gaelic ceann meaning headland, extremity. Similarly mor and mhor are the anglicised and Gaelic words for big.

The suffix val, abhal, aival, aval must all mean hill, not valley as might have been thought, but the exact root to this is unclear. It is encouraging to know that the Dutch for hill is huevel. When I discussed this with a Gaelic speaker and compared the word for hill in Dutch with the word for hill in French, colline, he immediately suggested a link with the Cuillins in Skye.

It would be the task of an expert to examine all the names in this walk but a few will give a flavour of their fascination. Clachan is straightforward Gaelic for stones. Mollinginish comes from moll meaning shingly beach and innis meaning green pasture, which is a good description of this spot in Harris. The suffix innis(h) is common. The hills An Coileach and Bulabhall are named more poetically; the former

v

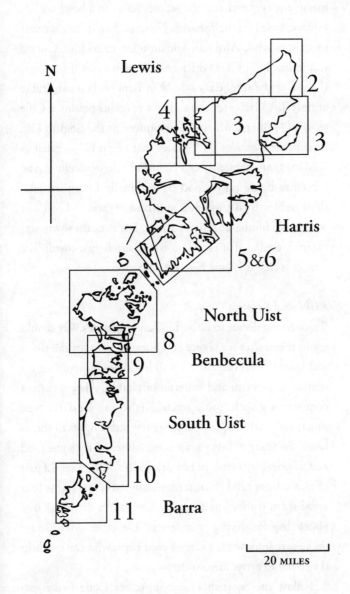

Figure 1 The Outer Hebrides –
key to sketch maps by chapter number

means the cockerel and the second refers to a bowl both, I assume, based on their shapes. Na Creachan in Lewis refers to scallops while Aird nan Sruban refers to cockles. Cnoc a Lin means hill of flax which makes me wonder if Linoclet, the site of the secondary school in Benbecula means ridge of flax. The Gaelic for the cell of a religious person is Cille as in Cille Bharra which is pronounced as the English kill. It makes me wonder if all places that begin Kil— (such as Kildonan) are named after a chapel or religious cell; maybe a beehive house once stood there. Finally I turn to Baleshare in North Uist which is an island of sand and machair with many houses and rich pasture. Baile means town, siar means west. So if it is west-town where is east-town? The answer is that it is now beneath the waves.

Risks and Safety

Readers who decide to walk the Outer Hebrides Way should equip themselves for severe conditions – plan for the worst and hope for the best. Stout walking shoes or boots are essential, as is warm and waterproof clothes. Always carry a compass, a whistle and a torch. Nights can be dark, even moon and starlit nights. There are few street lights in the islands. Be ready to bivvy on moors. Always carry some food and, if possible, a flask of hot drink. In addition take a pair of plimsolls or sand shoes for crossing rivers and burns (but avoid them if they are in spate). And take a dry towel in a plastic bag for drying your feet on the other side. Always make sure someone is aware of your plans who can call help if you fail to arrive at your destination.

Follow the Scottish Outdoor Access Code (*www.outdooraccess-scotland.com*).

The Lewis Moors, Tong Sands, Morsgail Forest, Traigh Athmòr in North Uist, the North Uist Moor, the North and South Fords I single out as places for being especially careful.

Take particular care when crossing the tidal fords. They are no place for heroics. Never cross if you have been drinking alcohol. Do not carry a hip flask. Be aware of the risk of drowning. I mention Tong Sands, the North and South Ford and Traigh Athmòr in North Uist as places to be careful. Without reference to these places the book would be shorter and the experience of the walk less full. But they are places where walkers cross at their own risk. Islanders were pleased when roads and bridges provided safe and more reliable alternatives to the Fords

I advise all who follow me along these routes to be careful. Take no unnecessary risks and accept that you cross at your own risk. Assess the risks carefully and if in any doubt delay your crossing. Always make sure someone knows you are making the crossing.

At Tong Sands I say, "After considerable homework I was ready to make the crossing. I studied the tide tables published in the local paper, the *Stornoway Gazette*, and observed conditions on the sand. I planned to cross Tong Sands from Tong Farm to Culrigen on the outskirts of Stornoway exactly as shown on the 'Popular' edition of the OS maps.

"I judged that the tide was finally out. Many fears raced before my eyes; being lost in sinking sands, being drowned by a rapidly rising tide, getting lost on the sands and wandering out to sea. I reasoned that I would not lose my way if I could see Stornoway on the other side of the bay; I had my compass if fog clamped down. As for getting drowned, the tide was now out. It had gone out so slowly that it was difficult to believe that it would come in any more quickly. It would not come in unnoticed but I would be vigilant; the channels would fill first. I had no reason to doubt the stories of rapidly advancing tides. The rafts of saltings which formed the shore a few feet above the sands looked firm enough. They were high enough to keep me dry at high tide, low enough to scramble up if the tide came in very rapidly. The route marked on the map ran very close to this shore. I would be sensible, proceed with caution and go across without lingering."

The same advice applies on the North Ford. Of the North Ford I say, "I had been warned of the dangers of crossing the North Ford just as I had been warned of the dangers of using the ford across Tong Sands. Mindful of these warnings the first time I crossed the Ford I was guided by Mr Ewen Nicholson of Grimsay. Mr Nicholson and his father guided people across the Ford until the Causeway opened. I made the second crossing alone using Mr Nicholson's directions. It found it easier to cross with Mr Nicholson but common sense, caution, a compass and a willingness to correct mistakes got me though on my own. The road on its causeway is also obvious from the sands, close enough to provide a fall back. The sands are dry for 4 or 5 hours at low tide. It takes about a hour and a half to make the crossing."

Nevertheless I did get lost and had to use my compass to correct my path. It is as well to admit your mistakes quickly and try to correct them rather than keeping on doggedly.

On all four fords I had to cross stretches of water – two on the Tong Sands; one on Traigh Athmòr, three on the North Ford and two on the South Ford.

Web site: *www.outerhebridesway.org*

I have created a web site in order to encourage involvement with the cause of creating the Outer Hebrides Way. This will give up to date information about the creation of the

Way, and provide an opportunity for readers to add their own comments and experience about the route.

I welcome feed back from readers. If you prefer, write to me at the publisher's address, Northampton Square Ltd 26 Lewis Street, STORNOWAY, Isle of Lewis HS1 2JF

The web site also gives links to the Gatliff Hebridean Hostels Trust hostels (*www.gatliff.org.uk*) and other accommodation in the islands (*www.witb.co.uk*). Camping is possible in a lot of places. I have mentioned stores selling food on or near the route.

Historical overview of roads, tracks and ways in the islands

The basic framework of nineteenth century island tracks was metalled with pebbles but there were plenty of ways across moors and mountains, and threading from house to house through croft land. During the twentieth century the main tracks were covered with tarmac. However, many tracks and footpaths remained in use. Bit by bit, as the network of tar-macadam roads developed, tracks fell into disuse. In some places the tarmac road overlaid the previous track. In other places engineers were able to make straighter more level routes, thus separating the new route from the old. As the motor car became more pervasive, roads were straightened to provide quicker and more reliable communication, and this continues to the present day. Better communication has done a lot to ease the hard-ships of Hebridean life, especially in winter.

It is all too easy for visitors to see only the tarmac roads. Don't be distracted. There are plenty of walking opportunities. Look out for tracks apparently heading nowhere. Most of these tracks are of ancient provenance and remain in use perhaps running from beach to moor, or peat bank, perhaps going from a village to a now closed school. These are, how-ever, nothing like the "rolling English roads made by the rolling English drunkard", to use G K Chesterton's phrase. These are ways with a purpose. Following the way brings an understanding of their purpose. Understanding the purpose provides an insight into a former way of island life. I would not see everything in the islands from the timeless way but by walking I would better understanding what I did see.

This book proposes the creation of an Outer Hebrides Way using these ancient tracks and ways.

ACKNOWLEDGEMENTS

I WOULD LIKE to thank all who produce local historical or topographical guides in the islands. I acknowledge the guides to which I have referred at the appropriate point in the text. These are the unsung and often anonymous heroes of this work.

I would like to thank all those who gave me help and encouragement. I give especial thanks to Jim Crawford, David Fowler, Simon Fraser, Cllr Angus Graham, Bill Lawson, the late Angus MacAskill and his wife Mary, Cllr Alex MacDonald, Angie & Cathie Maclean, Robert MacGillivray, D R Macleod, George Macleod, Dr John MacLeod, John Murdo Morrison and Ewen Nicholson. All helped me to find parts of the route and answered my frequent questions. I also thank Nick Comfort, Jim Craigen, Stella Jardine, David Skinner and Dennis Turner and last but not least my dear wife Petra, for their consistent support and encouragement.

ACKNOWLEDGEMENT

Chapter 1

BEHOLD THE HEBRIDES!

The Outer Hebrides are Britain's far flung north-west frontier, an archipelago stretching over 120 miles north to south, thirty to sixty miles off the coast of Scotland. Islands of myth and mystery, of mists and dazzling sunsets across sparkling blue seas, of gentle machair and rugged mountains, home of a Gaelic speaking crofting people. A place of my heart; forever in my heart.

FOR MANY YEARS I had wondered if was possible to walk through the islands of the Outer Hebrides using old tracks and ways. Since my first visit in 1973 I had been smitten, had returned annually for many years, then several times every year, until I bought a home in North Uist. I had been to most islands but now I wanted to explore more methodically. I wanted to show how to understand the islands and to encourage others, especially young people on limited budgets, to make the physical and spiritual journey through the islands.

The ambiance of the islands, the warmth of the people, the diversity of the culture and the breathtaking scenery all attracted me but I had never been romantic about the place. Life in the isles is simple but tough. The islands are isolated from mainland Scotland, Scotland is a long way from London but even within the isles vast distances isolate place from place. Isolation shapes the character of the islands and their people. Isolation preserves its cultural and environmental quality.

I decided to start my journey at the Butt of Lewis the tip of the most northerly inhabited island. I aimed to walk to Heillanish its southern counterpart. Geography dictates that North Rona is the most northerly island 44 miles North North East of the Butt of Lewis and the island of Berneray, 6 miles south of Heillanish, is its most southerly. In practical terms these are distant horizons, just as St Kilda is the Hebrides' distant western horizon. There is always another horizon in the Outer Hebrides. The Butt to Heillanish would be my boundaries.

My journey tested the hypothesis that it is possible to walk the length of the Hebrides on existing tracks or quiet roads. But by definition a hypothesis may not be proven. As I made my way south the evidence quickly accumulated. Many ancient tracks and ways are still in existence, some are still in use. Many ancient navigational markers were still guiding travellers on these ways. So, if a new long distance footpath, the Hebridean equivalent of the West Highland Way or the Pennine Way, were to happen, it would not be a new creation but merely the linking of nearly forgotten extant ways.

The Beginning

On my first day in the islands, 22 August 1973, I walked from Tarbert to Rhenigidale Youth Hostel little aware of the significance of the route. The path was about three feet wide, well constructed with pebbles and small rocks but disappeared when it crossed slabs of rock. It took me through a hauntingly beautiful gaunt rocky mountainous landscape. Little did I realise that I was using the path in the timeless way, the way that countless generations of islanders had used the path.

I had been persuaded to visit the island on the strength of a lengthy conversation in the common room at Uig Youth Hostel. Two fellow hostellers had just returned from the Outer Hebrides on the afternoon ferry. The meeting occurred during a student youth hostelling tour around the west coast and inner islands of Scotland. My fellow hostellers had assured me that there was a Youth Hostel at Rhenigidale, a hostel like no other hostel in the United Kingdom. But it was not in the Scottish Youth Hostels Association handbook. "No, it's run by a small Trust. But it does exist" they emphasised.

As I climbed the first hill I watched the ferry, my only link with the outside world, steam out of East Loch Tarbert bound for Lochmaddy in North Uist. As far as the eye could see the place was deserted. There was no-one to ask for directions or reassurance. I had only been passed by one car on the two mile walk out of Tarbert, and that was travelling towards the ferry port, otherwise I might have hitched a lift. It was a cold, dank, misty day. (I came to learn that islanders call this "dreich"). I reached deep inside my soul for the confidence to continue.

After a seemingly endless climb the path reached the summit and began a gentle descent. Suddenly I was at the top of a steep cliff. The slope dropped away to sea level about 900 feet below. The path negotiated the cliff with twelve sensational hairpin bends, "the zig zags" in local parlance. After making the descent I sat for a while on the beach of that deserted sea loch in total silence. I was in awe. There was no going back. I knew not what lay ahead.

4

I left the beach and climbed out of the sea loch up a slope thankfully neither as high nor so precipitate as the other. The path took me up hill and down, around headlands, across timber bridges for another two or three miles before I reached a wooden garden gate. Like John Bunyan's Pilgrim in Pilgrims Progress I had reached my wicket gate. (Bunyan had long been a hero of mine as he hailed from my native Bedfordshire.) It was the end of my uncertainty but the beginning of my involvement with the islands. Beneath was a cluster of half a dozen dwellings, a village without a road. On the other side of the valley was the Hostel. Smoke rose from the chimney. Nirvana! The Youth Hostel did exist!

This path was Rhenigidale's lifeline. The alternative route was by sea from Scalpay or Tarbert. The postman walked out and back three times a week. The Hostel warden went to Tarbert for a drink at the Harris Hotel and walked back in the dark after the bar closed. During my five nights at the Hostel I heard stories of youthful hostellers with rucksacks being passed by sprightly seventy year old women carrying shopping bags.

During the 1980s, as I got more involved with the Trust that ran the Hostels, the Gatliff Trust, (I became a Trustee in 1980) I began to realise that the Rhenigidale path was not unique. I sensed that there was a network of tracks and ways in many other parts of the islands, a network which pre-dated the roads. This prompted me to collect walking guides but typically they pointed out the shortest route to a beach, beauty spot or mountain top. Or they suggested a one or two mile circular walk. In the age of the motor car the significance of the remaining network of ways usually went unnoticed in modern guide books.

Before the coming of the internal combustion engine the population of the islands had been denser and more widespread. Clearances, such as those in west Harris and west Barra, had changed the settlement pattern. So, in theory, an extensive network of tracks and ways must have existed. If this was the case, then long distance walks were possible. In other words, a much more viable proposition for the sort of person I thought was interested in the islands that a short circular walk.

For some time I pondered on how best to confirm my instinct. During the 1980s I lobbied the Islands' local authority to include the proposal for a long distance footpath, a Western Isles Way, in the Structure Plan. This they did in the 1988 edition when they committed themselves to "investigate the establishment of a long distance footpath route in the Western Isles". The updated Structure Plan published in 2003 commits the Council to "work with other appropriate agencies to identify a route suitable for development as a strategic path through the Western Isles." Structure Plans are statutory documents which provide a strategic planning framework for Councils. Henceforth they are obliged to consider all planning decisions in the context of the Plan. Some Local Plans (for example those for Barra and Vatersay, Uist and Benbecula) have included sections of the Western Isles Way in their proposals, the Council has yet to complete its plan for the route. The opening of the Harris Walkway in 2001 takes the project a step closer to reality as does the appointment of Access Officers by the Council in 2004.

Despite this success I was still some way from discovering the alternative network of tracks. In 1991 I spent several days at the National Map Library of Scotland using the excellent *Togail Tir Marking Time: The Map of the Western Isles* edited by Finlay Macleod. Logic dictated that old maps might offer clues to tracks and ways long since forgotten

The Ordnance Survey maps were the most fruitful source. The first edition of the Ordnance Survey 6" to the mile (1:2500) maps of the islands began appearing in 1853. The set was completed in 1881. Later editions of these maps added detail but it was patchy. Paths might be shown on one edition and disappear on the next, to reappear on successive editions. I was encouraged but knew that I had reached the point when field work could no longer be delayed.

Chapter 2

SEA AND MOOR

THE SEA DOMINATES Ness making itself felt from all angles by sight, sound and, in places, taste. Ness is the large triangle of land that forms Lewis's northern tip. The sea forms two of the three sides. The moor forms the other side pushing north into the centre of Ness. Its nose is the Butt of Lewis, immortalised by the Shipping Forecast in the days when the weather at Inshore Stations were reported. The Butt and the huge stacks of ancient black rock just off the coast are paragneiss of sedimentary origin.

The Butt is a rough introduction to the Hebridean seas, the most basic element which has fashioned the islands. The drama of the Butt is astonishing. The confluence of the Atlantic and the Minch creates a boiling wrath, its spectacular turbulence crashing against the Butt's black cliffs. Both the north-west Atlantic and the Minch have made their mark on the land. Both are unpredictable and inhospitable waters, but the Atlantic is different in scale and nature to the Minch. 3,000 miles to the west, across the Atlantic, is the New World, North America; 2,400 miles north is the Polar ice pack. Washed by the Gulf Stream, the Hebrides are largely immune from the more inhospitable influences of the Northern Atlantic and Arctic. The vastness of the Atlantic Ocean brings home the human scale of the townships dotted around the edge of the moor.

The Minch is the islands' channel of physical communication with the Scotland. Since the beginning of time the Minch has carried passengers to and from the Hebrides. Today domestic traffic mingles with travellers and tourists of every description. Occasionally the sea bears its teeth, cutting the islands off from Scotland.

Travel across the Atlantic from the islands is less frequent. More often than not these have been the journey with no immediate hope of landfall, or return. They have been journeys to a new world, a better life. But for all its scale and menace the Atlantic has also presented an alternative route to the islands; the Vikings from the north, pilgrims from the south brought the Celtic vision of Christianity. The influence of these travellers is still strong on the Outer Hebrides. When crossing the Minch the Hebridean landfall is always a moment of awe and relief. Its sight brings anticipation, the greeting of an old friend. The many miles of endless motorways followed by the last couple of hundred miles of darkened Highland roads to the ferry port, perchance a deer caught in the headlights, are made worthwhile by landfall and disembarkation in this different world.

Even today the Minch is capable of isolating the islands from the mainland despite the larger more powerful vessels which ply back and forth. The necessity of a sea crossing impinges on the cost of goods sold in island shops and on island produce sent to the mainland. Petrol, for example, costs several pence per litre more than on the mainland.

Island life has always been intertwined with the sea. In the past crofting and fishing were an ideal combination. The collection of seaweed, kelp, for the production of iodine and other chemicals was another product of the sea, as is the

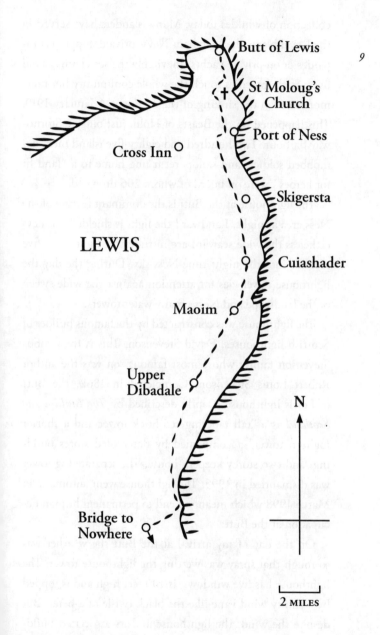

Figure 2 Butt of Lewis to the Bridge to Nowhere, North Tolsta

collection of winkles today. Many islanders have served in the Royal Navy, the Merchant Navy, private shipping companies or on private yachts. Inevitably the sea claims island lives. Such tragedies touch the whole community but none more so than the sinking of the *Iolaire* on 1 January 1919. This happened on the Beasts of Holm just outside Stornoway harbour. Two hundred and eighty-five island men, demobbed soldiers and sailors returning home to a "land fit for heroes", were on board of whom 206 drowned.

The lighthouse at the Butt is the dominant feature of the Ness area at night. Landward the light is shielded but nevertheless the wide seaward arc intrudes the light every five seconds into the night time Ness sky. During the day the lighthouse tower vies for attention against the wide sweep of the landscape and Ness's many water towers.

The lighthouse was constructed by the famous builder of Scottish lighthouses, David Stevenson. This is the famous Stevenson family whose most famous son was the author Robert Louis Stevenson. Completed in 1862, the Butt of Lewis lighthouse is aptly described by *The Buildings of Scotland* as a "tall tapering red-brick tower and a shorter foghorn tower" accompanied by flat roofed stores buildings and two storey keeper's house. The separate fog tower was dismantled in 1995. The lighthouse went automatic in March 1998 which meant an end to permanent human occupation at the Butt.

On the day of my arrival at the Butt the weather was so rough that spray was wetting the lighthouse tower. The lighthouse has five windows, is 100 feet high and is topped by a jaunty wind vane like the black twisle of a beret. But despite the wind, the lighthouse and its associated buildings, white painted walls etched with brown, looked gay.

How welcome this light must be to seafarers. One can

only wonder at the number of lives it has saved. How can one ever again feel dispassionate when listening to the Shipping Forecast? When I was a research student I always listened to the Shipping Forecast at half past midnight on Radio 4.

Alone at the Butt, the howl of the wind and the roar of the crashing sea came as a shock. It was deafening. The second shock was to find that the cliffs come right up beneath the lighthouse. Below a huge wave boiled and crashed into the rocks. I recoiled. My ambitious ideas about walking through the Hebrides flashed before my eyes. They seemed frail, ridiculous compared to these overwhelming physical forces.

On this sober note I turned south to start my journey. I retraced my footsteps along the asphalt road to the croft houses of Eoropie.

It is roughly 120 miles to Vatersay as the crow flies but I knew I would walk much further. My preparatory map work had sketched a route through nine islands about twice that distance. I aimed to avoid the main roads by finding old tracks and ways but I knew that this would not be easy in some places where the road dominates.

The Butt is some distance from the scattered settlements of Ness but I soon returned to the junction where the bus from Stornoway had dropped me an hour or so earlier. As soon as I turned south the wind seemed less menacing but it was still strong. Close to the junction is the ancient Temple of Eoropie, St Moloug's Church, outside which is a large decorated Celtic cross. (The church became my spiritual point of departure.)

I took advantage of the silence. In this age of constant communication silence is little heard, too often shunned or avoided. In the Hebrides silence is everywhere, broken only by the sounds of nature and one's own thoughts. Why yearn for that phone call to break the silence of daily life when so much more can be built from reflection?

The Temple had provided me with retreat and refreshment. There are few written records but in the Middle Ages it is known that the church was a place of pilgrimage for the sick and insane. Those with sores could seek relief by proxy, by sending an emissary with a plaster or wooden model of their wound. The insane, however, had to come in person and spend the whole night in the church. If the arduous journey and the rituals of the visit did not cure them they were declared incurably insane. Mental illness is still frightening. It is the most stigmatising of illness that can strike anyone especially gifted young people. It was a surprise to learn of its connection with the Temple.

The building was restored in the early part of the twentieth century. The official guide in the church says that since then it has been "firmly secured within the Episcopal Church of Scotland." Less orthodox forms of worship were "banished". During the 1990s St Moloug's was brave enough to appoint the first woman Minister in the islands, the Revd Barbara Morrison. What is interesting is that here in the midst of a deeply Protestant island with its plain churches with whitewashed interiors and varnished woodwork, and straight-forward liturgy to match, is an old stone built church still displaying its Celtic and Catholic origins.

The church door clanked shut as I left leaving me, again, to the wind. I walked back to the road along the path through the fields with their parallel fences marking each succeeding apportionment of land and turned south east along the B8014 towards the Port of Ness. The road was quiet. I walked past the crofts of Eoropie to Five Penny Ness. I caught glimpses of the artefacts of peoples' lives, so different to the lives we have grown accustomed to in the south, lived close to both land and sea. An open topped fishing boat, red and white, (the first of many laid up boats, large and small, in the district in a variety of gay colours), a tractor and trailer, a car on blocks. I saw people going about their everyday lives, working the fields on tractors, struggling with rams, herding ewes. Most crofters were accompanied by their black and white collies.

I smelled peat burning. I could hear a Harris Tweed weaver in his shed, the traditional metal loom clack, clack, clacking. Over the field I saw the Ness Football Club Social club. At night, no doubt, the yellow Tennants lager sign glows bright across the fields. The Club has removed the need for the bothans, illegal drinking haunts in roughly converted old buildings which were once common in the area.

Eoropie achieved national notoriety for its bothans in 1977 when a police raid led to a Court case in Stornoway. So many members of the public wanted to attend that extra seating had to be provided. A police officer told the Sheriff he had counted "fourteen full bottles of whisky; two bottles partially full; eleven empty whisky bottles; one full bottle of rum; one partially full bottle of rum; 415 full cans of beer and lager; twenty-two partially full cans; sixty-eight empty cans; four full eleven-gallon containers of beer; one partially full container; five empty containers – as well as a bucket containing 1,133 can top rings." On the basis of this evidence the Chief Inspector "came to the conclusion that this was a place that was used for drinking excisable liquor."

This exchange always makes me smile. Islanders have always had a disdain for authority, petty bureaucracy and regulation whose application offers little or no apparent assistance in mastering the forces of daily life. It also speaks volumes for the interdependencies of island life. After the raid the police gave the drinkers lifts home in their van. The drinkers had to sit on top of the impounded booty.

Ness enchants with its compactness. Its isolation from the rest of Lewis creates a closeness of community. Today it is an active and lively place complete with Community Council, Historical Society, active churches and football club, even a pub, the Cross Inn. The mix of house styles is testimony to the centuries old natural processes of rejuvenation rooted in a close relationship between domestic life and the life of the croft. The old houses, built almost entirely of stone, contrast with the newer brick or kit bungalows. Most traditional houses are two storeys with storm or dormer windows built into the roof. Others are converted black houses, now with corrugated or bitumen roofs. Some houses have extensions tacked on, side or back or both, presenting a house with multiple roof levels. Some have neat front porches. The stonework of only a minority of houses is painted, thus avoiding the treadmill of repainting demanded by the Hebridean weather. Mixed in are a good number of empty houses. Derelict houses stand until they fall, so it is possible to see houses in various states of decay, roofs staved in, walls collapsed. Some are piles of rubble covered in stinging nettles over-run by sheep and rabbits. Hebridean custom seems to dictate that houses are abandoned with their contents intact. Fallen walls reveal intimate glimpses of life, hand made chairs and tables mixed with shop bought chests of drawers and beds, even a few ornaments left on the mantelpiece. Perhaps their owners will return. The return home of distant relatives is a widespread hope in the islands.

Each house has an outhouse or two. One may be the former stone built black house, others may be modern stores built of solid looking dark green zinc. There are plenty of mobile homes, also known down south as 'caravans'. Some provide a temporary home whilst a house is built or renovated. A few are let to summer holiday makers. Some are providing permanent homes. Each winter the gales mangle a few, their twisted remains left where they fall. Here and there cars rust quietly, some on blocks. Many are kept for spare parts. Tractors and trailers abound. Most back yards are strewn with a miscellany of agricultural machinery. I particularly like the old vans pressed into use as make shift outhouses. Most still display their original livery albeit faded. On my walk to Knockaird I passed a green van with the word "Co-operative" down its side in white letters on a red background There are also a fair number of old coaches, mostly Duple coaches but some older, used as green-houses or for more general storage. In South Uist an enterprising chap has converted two of these buses for use by tourists.

The sweet smell of burning peat reinforces the cosy fireside image of the islands. Peat is abundant and has been burned in the islands for centuries. Large peat stacks appear behind many Hebridean homes in the summer and shrink as winter progresses. But the practice of burning peat is in decline as the physical demands of peat cutting are weighed against the monetary cost of alternative fuels.

As I climbed the hill at Knockaird a real bonus, the discovery of an old black house still with its thatch netted down. Thatched houses are part of the islands' historic triumph over nature. However, many islanders want to forget that past. Perhaps they are rueful about the way their forebears once lived in such dwellings with their parged floors and soot encrusted roofs, but I believe that this is a tradition which should be celebrated. It speaks volumes for Hebridean tenacity and adaptability to the environment.

I walked to the main road, the A857, and turned left

down into the Port of Ness a pretty harbour. The harbour is the scene of the annual autumn cull of young gannets, known locally as Guga. According to John Beatty in his book, *Sula. The seabird hunters of Lewis*, in September every year "ten chosen men (of Ness) slip quietly away on the evening tide, bound for Sula Sgeir, to hunt the guga and keep faith with the past." Sula Sgeir is an island 40 miles north of the Butt of Lewis. Salted guga are sold to a ready market on the quay-side, as they are regarded as a great delicacy. The adult gannet, a magnificent white bird with a six foot wingspan and yellow head, is a fearsome sight when seen diving into the sea at close quarters. It is a protected species but the Protection of Birds Act, 1954 was amended to permit the Nessmen to hold to tradition and take 2000 birds per year.

I turned south to walk to Skigersta from where I planned to go on to the moor. I did not have to walk far before I got to the junction with the B8015, the road which leads directly to the moor. Conveniently, at the corner, there is a large brown road sign with white English and Gaelic directions to the start of the Tourist Board walk across the moor. Just before the turn I encountered a fine example of local humour. A house had four golden lions standing sentinel as gate post decorations. I was reliably informed that they all have eyes from old teddy bears. (A year or so later it appears that the lions have gone.) Just after, at Adabroc, the land had risen sufficiently to give an excellent view of the sea to the north across the Port of Ness. Seamlessly I passed from one township to another as I walked towards the moor.

The term township is common in the islands but is unfamiliar elsewhere in the British Isles. It denotes a settlement in a crofting area. These settlements are often dispersed with croft houses built on their crofts. The term was first defined by the Napier Commission, a Royal Commission set up in 1883 which looked into conditions in the crofting communities. They said it was a district or group of crofts called by a separate name. The townships of this part of Ness are formed by rows of houses along the road.

As I passed through Eorodal a more dispersed pattern re-emerged. So too did further amusing artistic displays on top of gate posts. One had chosen the menhir as its gate post theme. Each post displayed a collection of small flat stones pointing sky-wards. Next door the theme was an old fashioned white painted lantern with two white horses made from sheet metal. Art was mixed with utility: a black box on the gate post with a white milk bottle painted on it, another with the word "Post" in red letters.

They were all eclipsed by an amazing statue about three feet high in the garden of a house in Adabroc. This depicted a plump but squat fish, atop a wave. Its mouth was open to display its large teeth, with a large duck on its head peering into the mouth. Two smaller birds stand on its tail.

A detail of this sculpture is displayed on the cover of a book of short stories, *Special Deliverance*, by Donald S Murray. He told me the sculpture was created by Ian Brady. "It was one of six post boxes commissioned by An Lanntair (the art gallery in Stornoway) and sponsored by the Post Office in about 1992. They were erected in various places round the islands to be used for post, newspaper deliveries etc. No real serious purpose – but in its ideas it reflects island life, particularly wild life and fishing. It was made of fibre-glass resin with stone. It was also stained with peat and lightly painted. I borrowed it for my book for two reasons – a pun on Special Delivery (Post Office) and also the 'deliverance' of a bird feeding a fish."

I walked past the junction with Skigersta Cross Road.

From here I could see the open moor. It looked dank and uninviting. In most seasons the Lewis Moor is green, brown, massive and mysterious, undulating into the distance as far as the eye can see. The road ran level on a well built embankment. At first I thought this was the northern end of the 'Leverhulme road', Lord Leverhulme's road from Ness to Tolsta. But the road, and its embankment, is shown on the 1853 6" OS map.

The final township before the moor is Skigersta, "*Sgiogarstaigh*" in Gaelic sign. It is partly clustered on the top of the cliff some way north west of the road I was walking. The fields on both sides of the road gave way to rougher vegetation, with tufts of osier. Further along I saw a large dog 'sleeping' in front of a house. It found me far too interesting to ignore, gave up its pretence of sleep and cantered down to the road for a closer look. I was glad it did not jump the fence. The last few houses before the moor, neatly renovated and pebble dashed were all too civilised compared with the wild moor beyond. To the south I could see the television transmitter on Airigh na Gaoithe. It was erected to provide BBC2 and ITV to the area in 1976 well after most people down south had taken both channels for granted.

The Moor

The Lewis Moor represents 80% of the land surface of Lewis north of the A858 Stornoway to Callanish road, 230 square miles in all. It rises from the coast to a ridge at an average height of 150 metres but there are higher peaks. The twin peaks of Muirneag rise to over 240 metres. To the west the highest of the three Bragar hills, Beinn Bhragair, rises to 261 metres. Nearer to Stornoway another clutch of hills rises of which Beinn Mholach is 292 metres. Peat covers the surface to an average depth of 1.5m. As well as the television mast on Airigh na Gaoithe there is also a mast in the south on Eitseal (223 m), close to the A858.

In the 1980s a Nature Conservancy Council study observed, "The main part of the peat land landscape, especially in its extreme form in Lewis, is not generally considered to be aesthetically attractive but the sheer barrenness of some areas and the impression of wildness may be powerful." Martin Martin said in 1707 that Lewis was so named because "in Irish language it signifies water lying on the surface of the ground which is proper to this island because of the great number of fresh water lakes that abound in it."

In crofting terms the moor is 'Common Grazing'. As such it is far from barren. It is an integral part of the crofting system used for the summer grazing of sheep and a source of peat for fuel. Sheep are turned out in spring, collected once or twice during the summer for shearing, inoculation or market. So vast is the moor that herding has to be done collectively by townships. All the crofters of a township and their dogs take to the moors on an appointed day to round up the township sheep. Once corralled in a fank, the local name for a sheep fold or cluster of fenced enclosures, they are sorted into individual flocks, re-united with their owners, dipped or sheared, prepared for market or returned to the croft. All sheep carry ear and paint marks. What the visitor sees on the backs of sheep are not random splodges of red, green or blue paint. Each mark is distinct. Indeed, they are sometimes more distinct that the names of their owners. Some island historical societies have produced directories of sheep marks. These come in handy for distinguishing between their crofter owners with identical names.

I had heard crossing the Lewis Moor described as one of most arduous walks in the Outer Hebrides. I found only one historical reference to a walking expedition on the moor. This was in John Wilson Dougal's 1937 book *Island Memories*. In 1990 the *Stornoway Gazette*, however carried a story about a local sixth former from the Nicholson Institute who had made the crossing. Subsequently he and his colleagues produced *The Alternative Guide to Lewis and Harris* published in 1991.

The Tourist Board way marked a route and published a guide in 1995. It starts at a small car park beyond Skigersta and runs in a circuitous way to Tong. Alongside the car park was a large interpretative board showing the route as printed in the Tourist Board leaflet. The car park was positioned at the point where the asphalt road gives way to a well made levelled pebble based track. The pebble based track took a fairly straight line high above the surrounding moor. It ran about two miles to Cuiashader, a settlement of shielings or summer dwellings within the Abhainn Dubh valley.

Each of the townships surrounding the moor has at least one well made track onto the moor starting on or near the beach. Often referred to as the 'township road', these tracks are well built with rocks, pebbles and shells from the beaches. The course of the township road will not necessarily be straight because this depends on the nature of the croft apportionments and natural obstacles. The straighter their lines, the straighter the township road. All such roads inevitably peter out, some near an area of peat cuttings, others at a flat area or slab of rock where a tractor and trailer can turn. "We used to walk up the township road until it gave out, and then continue on across the moor" I was told by a local friend, recalling how he used to walk from place to place across the moor. I guess these trips were common place at one time but no records were kept.

There were a good number of shielings at Cuiashader

many still in use as weekend retreats. They present a variety of building styles, including some built in a tough ply-wood called yacht board. I noticed one shieling with a bright orange hatch door in the gable end. Another had an 'H' shaped chimney pot. I peeped through the window of one. I could see a cosy scene: an arm chair, a bed, a home made pink painted upright chair, whisky glasses, a lamp, gas rings and a small gas cooker. Here and there books and newspapers were scattered.

The moor is dotted with shielings but beyond Cuiashader the majority are derelict. Shielings are the clue to the summer economy of the moor. There are plenty of stories about 'shieling life'. Perhaps the best known is Donald MacDonalds's book *Lewis A history of the island*. Most shielings were built like the old 'black' houses and could shelter milch cows and calves on cold nights. The *tigh Earraich*, spring dwelling, made it possible for stock to be sent to the moors earlier than usual, particularly when fodder was scarce after a bad winter. It had only one wooden door and there were windows on the wall-tops. The beds were built into thickened end walls. The stone bed platform was raised about three feet from the clay floor and a stone coping in front of it kept the bedding from falling out. The side walls contained recesses, 'milk presses,' where the milk was stored. At the end of the season it was common practice to remove the turf roof to avoid damage to the timbers.

Shieling life remained unchanged for centuries. W Anderson Smith described the life over 125 years ago. Seton Gordon describes the same life in the 1920s, as does Arthur Geddes in the 1950s. Stone was plentiful but roof timbers were scarce so had to be carefully conserved. It is not surprising, therefore, that all old shielings are found unroofed today.

South of the Abhainn Dubh valley the track deteriorated quickly becoming a narrow wet dirt track. Even this track petered out in Bilascleiter a little under a mile further on. From here I could see the Tourist Board's markers going east towards the cliffs in a wide loop. I was seeking a more direct route south. From Bilascleiter I tried to head south east but found myself crossing a dank bog from which I had no choice but to retreat. Not a good start. I could see one of the Tourist Board's marker posts returning their route from the cliffs to the side of a deeply incised bay. The headland on the southern side of this bay is called Leum Langa. I got to this post without difficulty and turned inland along the valley of the burn running into the bay.

The first edition of the OS 6" survey of the Lewis Moor, published in 1853, shows an intermittent track across the moors from Skigersta to Tolsta but I did not know if I would find this track on the ground. I was confident, however, that if a route had existed in 1920 Lord Leverhulme would have used it as the basis for his route from Skigersta to Tolsta. It seemed likely that the 1853 track had been engulfed by the moor. As I walked towards Maoim I believed I was close to this route.

Maoim turned out to be a real gem, the charming sight of three roofless stone shielings built in black house style exactly as described by W Anderson Smith in 1875. Small ferns dotted the walls. At one end, the building had a ledge on both sides, I assume for sitting, and at the other end a large cavity in the wall for the bed. I tried it for size. I guess it was about the same size as the box beds at the black house at Arnol so I assume people must have been smaller in those days.

The shielings lay on a carpet of soft sward, mosses and lichens, alongside a gently babbling brook. It was a peaceful spot sheltered from the wind. A tiny chocolate brown jenny wren flew low across the grass to the lower ruin.

There were numerous Tourist Board posts beyond Mao-im. A scrap of track appeared and crossed the stream by a broken plank bridge. As I crossed the bridge I saw a wooden post on top of the valley side. Thinking it was the next Tourist Board post I walked to it only to find I was mistaken. The post was unpainted and roughly hewn. Tourist Board posts are neatly cut painted green with a yellow or pink band around their top. This prominent post was obviously a marker post but what was it marking? It had given me line of sight up the steep convex slope. At the time I was a little irritated but later I was to realise the true significance of these marker posts.

From this 'unofficial post' I could see the Tourist Board route going off to the south east but again making a detour to take the route close to the cliff top. I decided to press on to the top of the hill along this new alignment. The map showed buildings at Dibadale both on the cliffs as well as inland. I continued up a gentle slope to the top of a low hill and was rewarded with a view forward to Dibadale and far to the south to Tolsta Head.

The coastal scenery at Dibadale is spectacular. There are high cliffs teaming with birds and a stack in the bay of twisted and gnarled red rock topped with strips of yellow lichen. It was alive with birds. Seals swam in the clear waters of the bay. Inland, to the east, two burns joined in a rocky gorge and flowed to the sea through a deep valley. The only building I could see in the area was a modern shieling made of yacht board. I walked along the top of the valley to Upper Dibadale where I found the remains of several stone shielings just as at Maoim. Dibadale or Dibiodal in Gaelic was just as charming and peaceful in its location on the northern side of a wide valley. The stream meandered across this valley before going into the gorge.

At Upper Dibadale I was back close to the line of the route shown on the 1853 map but there was no evidence of this route on the ground. I crossed the valley and climbed its southern side. From the top I could see a large post about half a mile to the south. This post was not of the Tourist Board route. I could see that route continuing much closer to the cliffs. I decided to walk to this post. Maybe this was all the evidence I would find of the 1853 route. It turned out to be another tall bare piece of wood about 4' 6" high on a small but prominent hill. It was clearly a marker post but was not associated with any visible track. This was not an old fence or tethering post.

From this post I continued south west walking more or less parallel to the Tourist Board route along the cliffs. This took me along the western side of Loch Sgeirachna na Creige Brist. Both the *Alternative Guide* and the Tourist Board leaflet say it is home to monster trout. These myths make me smile.

After my first encounter with bog south of Bilascleiter the moor had been soggy and bumpy but passable. After Maoim the ground seemed to get more undulating and south of Dibadale had become wave like. These were not major undulations which showed on a map; rather the surface of the moor resembled a static brown sea. Negotiating each 'wave' was enough to break my stride. Further south still the troughs were so deep that my line of sight was cut by the ridge.

Walking in a straight line was good in theory but it took me across another boggy area. I quickly realised that the light coloured areas were wetter than the darker tufts. I made for a patch of darker tufts at the head of Loch Sgeirachna na Creige Brist and found that I had correctly reasoned that this would be an area of firmer ground. I felt the ground shift beneath my feet as I walked across rafts of turf on top of the soggy mass. At times my stick sank several feet through the soft surface. This line eventually took me back to the Tourist Board route but it was not long before the Tourist Board offered another detour to the coast, this time to Dun Othail, the site of a brutal revenge famed in Gaelic history.

I continued on a more direct route. There were a lot of posts in this area in addition to the Tourist Board posts. The others were rough unpainted pieces of wood. Some were so large that they would have required considerable effort to transport and erect on the treeless moor. But what were they marking? Had they been left by Leverhulme's surveyors? Or were they marking the route shown on the 1853 map? I walked to an old post on a rise which was definitely on the 1853 line but, again, there was no sign of a track. I became convinced that the presence of the post was evidence enough of a route. Eighteenth or nineteenth century passage would have been on foot or horseback which would have caused little permanent disturbance. In this sort of terrain and weather conditions any evidence of such passage would quickly disappear. When I got to this post I reckoned that I had entered Stornoway Parish.

From this post I could see my route off the moor going directly to the south south west past a ridge in the peat shaped with two nicks. Beyond the peat ridge I found a flattened strip wide enough to be an old track; an exciting discovery. To the south the houses of Tolsta were visible on a distant hill. Then, at the next ridge south, I came upon an oblong area cut out of the peat (about 30 by 10 feet) as if in preparation for the foundations of a road. Beyond this were two similar rectangular sections filled with angular grey rocks. These were definitely old road foundations. A flock of grouse or partridge flew by noisily.

The guide books all say that Leverhulme's road-making efforts stopped at the 'Bridge to Nowhere'. This was still at least a mile further south. If this earth and stone work was not related to the Leverhulme road it must be associated with a previous route, maybe the 1853 route. Either way it was exciting.

To the south of the exposed road foundations the track crossed a burn, the Abhain na Cloich, over a rough concrete channel. The *Alternative Guide* calls this a 'concrete block' but I wondered if it was a bridge foundation. South of the burn a well made track continued south to the Bridge to Nowhere around the seaward side of a spur. The burn I had crossed at the 'concrete block' plunged over a waterfall into a deep valley before entering the sea. At first the road was high on the side of this valley. After passing through a wide gap blasted in a huge rock threaded with a fine band of granite, the track was on a slope which went directly down to the sea.

There were spectacular views, first of the Abhainn na Cloich valley and the cliffs to the north, then of Horga-bost beach and Tolsta Head to the south. The Abhainn na Cloich valley was picturesque, full of heather and bracken sprinkled with slender grey green leafed trees. The cliffs and sea teamed with birds, gulls of various types, shags or cor-morants.

Just to the east of the Bridge to Nowhere the track joined a track coming off the moor. Map work confirmed that this is the southern end of the 1853 route. From the junction, travelling north, it goes over the spur and crosses the Ab-hainn na Cloich by a ford. It then bends round the side of the wide Abhainn na Cloich valley to meet the earth and stone works. This lends credibility to the view that the foundations may have been part of the 1853 way rather than the Leverhulme road.

'The Bridge to Nowhere', as it is known locally, is said to be the last piece of the Leverhulme Road to have been completed before all work ended in 1920. As I approached from the north all I could see were its concrete balustrades. However, from the south, the open front of the bridge is visible. It is a fine, sound, structure crossing the deep gorge of the Garry River.

The 1853 map shows the previous route crossing the Garry River by a ford but it also shows a foot bridge closer to the sea. The map marks this crossing as a "prospective bridge". One of the bridge stanchions is still to be seen on the south side of the river.

The history of the Leverhulme Road and Garry Bridge, the Bridge to Nowhere, is described in Nigel Nicolson's book *The Lord of the Isles*. Nicolson records that nineteenth century roads in the islands were "surprisingly numerous" but their surfaces were neglected during the Great War. Crofters either travelled on foot or with a pony and cart. It took a whole day to cross Lewis on foot. Several more distant townships had no road at all. Lord Leverhulme agreed to improve the roads as part of his general improvements to the island. He also conceived the ambitious plan to link North Tolsta to Skigersta. Work started in April 1919 at both ends simultaneously "more to give employment in these two districts than to fill any desperate need as it would shorten the journey to Stornoway by only two miles in twenty six and pass through wholly uninhabited country." On 12 May 1920 work ceased abruptly with only a dozen men retained to complete the Garry Bridge. Consequently the Bridge to

Nowhere is seen throughout Lewis as the symbol of Lever-hulme's unyielding attitude to the islands.

Reaching the Bridge to Nowhere was an important moment. It meant that I had crossed the Lewis Moor. The crossing had been strenuous but not "impassable" even though the terrain had been more varied than expected. The whole experience had been exhilarating; enough for one day.

Chapter 3

THE LAND OF HOPE

CROSSING THE LEWIS Moor gave me confidence that I could find a route through the islands but I was puzzled about the next section, how to reach Stornoway. The B895 appeared to be the only route. It swept down the coast from North Tolsta to Newmarket on the outskirts of Stornoway. Walking along the road did not appeal. The old maps confirmed the obvious; the road had taken the only direct land route to Stornoway. The road ran through a strip of cultivated land of varying width between the moor and the Minch. As I set off south I was ready to accept the inevitable, that I would have to use the B895, but I hoped to find an alternative.

It is just over a mile from the Bridge to Nowhere to the cattle grid that marks the beginning of Tolsta township. The single track road skirts a long stretch of sand called Horgabost Beach. According to the *Alternative Guide* Horgabost was the venue of Sixth form revels in the late 1980s. Happy days. I smiled. I walked through Tolsta past the Post Office (which I noticed also sold a few groceries). There was no traffic. The contemporary OS map shows tracks crossing the moor south of the village. To reach these tracks I took a minor road which diverged from the B895 half way through the village and climbed a hill. Over my shoulder I got a fine view of the moor and the cliffs past Dibadale to the north. To the south the sky was growing lighter I took this as a good omen. As I breasted the hill Tiumpan Head, the tip of the Eye Peninsula, came into view some miles to the south east. Its white lighthouse stood out against the black rock of the Head. Behind it the villages of Point laid out across the Peninsula were splashed in sunshine.

I picked up one of the tracks just south of the village. It took me sharp to the north east past a gaunt derelict building. At a bend in the track I took a lush wide green track which joined another township road and then over the moor. After it petered out I picked my way across the peat cuttings for a short distance until I joined a short track which eventually took me down to the B895.

I rejoined the B895 road at the southern end of Tolsta. As I walked along a wide verge I found fragments of the previous asphalt road on top of a low embankment. This pleased me as it kindled the hope that I would, after all, find an alternative route to Stornoway. Later, south of Glen Tolsta, my hope was fulfilled. From the top of Glen Tolsta, just beyond the pagoda-like water treatment building with its red painted windows, I could see the old road going east around the hill whilst the new road took a straighter course south by cutting through the moor. It was a portent of things to come. I found the new road threaded by the old road for most of its length to Gress. Later I found both roads marked on the 1997 edition of the OS 1:50,000 map.

The old road proved to be an excellent walk gliding along the surface of the moor. Modern engineering technology had allowed the new road to take a more level route producing a series of cuttings beneath the moor's surface. The new road was the only alternative for only one section of

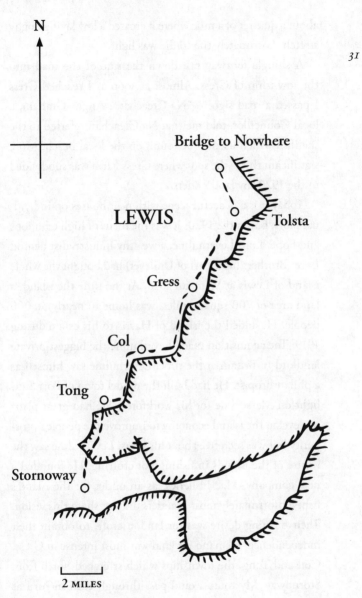

Figure 3   Tolsta to Stornoway

about a quarter of a mile where it crossed a low laying boggy stretch. Fortunately the traffic was light.

A shingle footway ran down the side of the road into the township of Gress. Almost as soon as I reached Gress I passed a road sign to "Na Creachan". Angus Graham, a local Councillor, told me that Na Creachan referred to the shellfish which used to be found on the local beach. More significant this is the spot where Gress Farm was subdivided in the 1920s by land raiders.

Today it is a peaceful scene with neat houses on individual plots, but in the 1920s it was the focus of high emotions and hope. Lord Leverhulme, a wealthy industrialist behind Lever Brothers (now part of Unilever) had bought the whole island of Lewis at Whitsun 1918. At the time the island, a land area of 700 square miles, was home to nearly 30,000 people. He added the island of Harris to his estate during 1919. The acquisition made Leverhulme the biggest private landlord in Britain at the time. Leverhulme saw himself as a philanthropist. He had built the model town of Port Sunlight on Merseyside for his workforce. He had great plans to develop the island economy to improve the people's prosperity but was secretive about his ideas. Leverhulme saw the future of the islands in fishing not crofting. He founded a new company, Mac Fisheries, as an outlet for the island's fish. Unfortunately most islanders did not share this vision. Their burning desire was for land, a croft, to obtain their independence. Demand for land was most intense in Gress, Coll and Tong, the townships which stretched north from Stornoway. My route would pass through each in turn as I approached Stornoway. This was just where Leverhulme had several large farms which he wished to use for milk and food production to support what he hoped would be the growing town of Stornoway. My own Doctoral researches had described the return of the unemployed to the land in England in the 1930s so I could well understand how these feelings provided the basis for conflict.

The Crofters Act 1886 had given crofters security of tenure. Crofters, small farmers were no longer required to move on at the whim of their landlord or at the expiry of their tenancy. However, little was done to increase the supply of crofts to match demand. The supply of crofts was still in the hands of the land owners. The Act also did nothing to improve the position of cotters and squatters. Cotters were landless people who dwelt on crofting land. Squatters occupied dwellings on parts the common grazing, marginal land and moor land. In other words the Crofters Act had not satisfied the demand for land it had merely dealt with the issue of security of tenure for one group of people who depended on the land for their livelihood. Leah Leneman's book about soldier and sailor land settlement in Scotland, *Fit for Heroes?*, describes this period of "highland land agitation and the intensity of demand" for land. She comments, "the struggle was bitter, for pitted against this belief was the inalienable right of any landowner in Britain to do as he wished with his land."

The historical antecedents of these issues in Scotland can be traced back to the Battle of Culloden in 1746 and the subsequent disintegration of the Clan as an economic and social system. Whereas the Clan system had guaranteed members of the Clan economic survival, because all Clan land had been held in common, the breakdown of the Clan system had concentrated ownership of the land in the hands of the former Clan chief. This could leave individual Clan members landless and homeless especially if the Clan chief sold on the land. Those who survived on the land did so entirely at the whim of the landlord with whom they may have no ties of Clan. Widespread poverty developed in the highlands and islands with consequent outward migration in the nineteenth century.

In 1916 land had been promised as a bounty for those who fought in the Great War. It was a traditional reward for victory in battle. Coming only thirty years after the Crofters Act this promise was taken seriously in the islands. During the General Election at the end of the War Lloyd George, the Prime Minister, spelt out his theme "a land fit for heroes" in an emotive speech in Wolverhampton. He said at one point:

> What is our task? To make Britain a fit country for heroes to live in ... there will be millions who will come back ... war has shown us ... the appalling waste of human material in this country ... (and) the enormous waste of the resources of our land ... Britain is a rich country so far as its soil is concerned. We import hundreds of millions of our supplies from abroad ... we can grow vast quantities of food in this country for which you have been dependent on imports, but you want a much more intelligent policy than that. The land must be cultivated to its full capacity ... a systematic effort must be made to bring a population back to the land.

The specific circumstances in Lewis made this promise inflammatory and it is not surprising that land raids followed. The law gave Leverhulme, as landlord, every right to take these decisions. He was motivated by good intentions. Leverhulme thought that fishing could provide a more certain income than crofting. He empathised with the islanders. After all he had succeeded from humble beginnings and he believed others could do the same by hard work and sac-rifice. He had built up immense wealth and power via Lever Brothers, a massive industrial concern producing soap and other consumer products at Port Sunlight near Liverpool. Leverhulme failed to recognise that good intentions could not appease the islanders' historical claim for land

The tragic loss of many returning island ex-servicemen on the *Iolaire* on 1 January 1919 intensified those feelings. After surviving brutal years in the trenches or on war ships and now the *Iolaire* disaster, Lewis men were not willing to resume their former lives. If they were to do so, for many, this meant continuing to live in their parents' home with their wives. They wanted their own croft, independence, a home of their own.

Despite the pressure to subdivide farms in Gress, Coll, and Tong, Leverhulme refused. In 1919 and 1920 the men of Gress and Coll took the matter into their own hands. At Gress they staked out plots on Leverhulme's farms includ-ing here at Na Creachan.

The buildings of Gress Farm lay a little further south along a further loop of old road isolated from the modern road. This took me past the old Gress Mill. The mill was large as judged by the extensive set of derelict buildings. The out-house opposite the farm was pretty with flowers in window boxes. A horse grazed in the enclosure between the old and the new road.

The verge along the modern road was wide enough to take me safely past Gress Cemetery. Graham, Maciver, Mackay, Macleod and Murray were among the names I saw on the tomb stones. Inside the cemetery is a small simple un-roofed stone building. This is an ancient chapel, the only ecclesiastical building in the Outer Hebrides dedicated to a Norwegian patron saint St Aulay Olaf.

The modern road crosses the Gress River by a new bridge. I wanted to cross the old bridge which remained on another cut off loop of old road. I jumped over the crash barrier on the embankment of the new bridge in order to cross by the old bridge. The Gress River water was peaty brown. Brown and black cows grazing on the braided saltings to the west formed a close backdrop.

Just south of the old bridge is a fine monument to the Gress Land Raiders. It consists of a rectangular central pillar enclosed by two brown round topped pillars. All three pillars are made of thousands of carefully selected local stones. They are said to be symbolic of Lord Leverhulme's attempts to fracture the crofting community. The pillars are set within an earth work, a circular mound of trenches and waves, symbols of the pledges given to the ex-service men. The memorial was erected in 1995 by Cuimhneachain Nan Gaisgeach, a local committee set up to commemorate the "land heroes". It was designed by the internationally acclaimed Scottish Artist Will Maclean and built by local stone mason Jim Crawford.

There is no commemorative booklet setting out the history of this memorial or the events which surrounded its construction. The Secretary of the Cuimhneachain Nan Gaisgeach, Matt Bruce, told me that this was in deference to local wishes. There are, however, commemorative booklets marking the unveiling of the other two memorials erected by Cuimhneachain Nan Gaisgeach in Point and Park.

Gress Bridge was the site of the historic confrontation on the land question between Leverhulme and the men of the area. Leverhulme met local men at the bridge and tried to reason with them. He made an impassioned plea asking them to abandon their hopes of land in favour of his scheme based on fishing. During one crucial passage he was interrupted by a local man in the crowd speaking in Gaelic. His speech was greeted with a rousing cheer from the crowd. Leverhulme asked for the man's comments to be translated into English. Not wishing to give offence, typical of Hebridean generosity to incomers, Leverhulme was told that much of it would not translate into English. Leverhulme's biographer, Nicolson comments that the crucial message was, nevertheless relayed to Leverhulme with the same intonation as the original speaker. The speaker had said, "we are not concerned with his fancy dream ... what we want is the land. The question is ... will he give us the land?" The effect was electric on both laird and landless. The raiders kept the land.

No doubt Leverhulme found the experience deeply disappointing. In the months that followed Leverhulme claimed that the land raids caused him to stop all development work on the islands including the road from Tolsta to Skigersta. However Nicolson reveals that whatever his declared motives, commercial difficulties at Lever Brothers had left him short of cash. When Leverhulme became completely disillusioned he decided to wash his hands of the islands and offered it to its inhabitants as a free gift. The only part of the island to accept was Stornoway Parish, which lead to the creation of the Stornoway Trust governed by a constitution which gave the electors of the Parish the power to elect the Trustees.

Elsewhere many thought Leverhulme was simply disposing of an unprofitable estate. Consequently the island was divided and sold privately, a pattern of ownership which prevailed for another eighty years. Only now, with the enactment of the Land Reform (Scotland) Act 2003 by the Scottish Parliament and the development of the community ownership model for estates, with sizeable public funds to back local decisions, are these historic decisions being overturned.

Incidentally the Land Settlement Association (LSA), the subject of my PhD thesis, created 1,100 small holdings on 21 co-operative estates for the unemployed in England. As many as 1,728 unemployed men were settled with their families on the estates, many ex-miners or ship builders. Some liked their new rural life but many, especially the wives, found it unrewarding and uncongenial. At the outbreak of war when the settlement of unemployed industrial workers was ended, 850 men were in occupation of land of smallholdings of whom 400 had tenancies. In 1948 the LSA became a part of the more orthodox statutory small-holdings policy offering the first rung on the farming ladder. The LSA was wound up by the Government in 1982.

At Gress Bridge my dilemma about the route south to Stornoway remained. There was no obvious alternative to the road. However, I noticed from the map that there was a footpath along the coast which, if passable, might allow me to avoid the road through Back and Coll. It started at the southern end of Gress beach a short distance south of the memorial.

I found a wide green track adjacent to a small green North of Scotland Water Authority box. The track went across a field and along the low cliff. Even after the path petered out there was enough space between the edge of the cliff and fences bounding the croft land to loop to the east of Back township. It was a rewarding walk. Initially the beaches were a mixture of sand and pebbles in massive piles. They gave way to wave cut platforms, square cut inlets, caves and a natural arch in a brown conglomerate rock full of large pebbles

I rounded the point, Gob Rubha Bhatasgeir, and came to

Brevig Harbour. The Harbour, down a steep embankment, was opened on 23 November 1995 by the late Christina MacDonald, a local lady renowned for her strong connections with the sea. At the spot there is a poignant memorial to "those fishermen of the district drowned in Broad Bay and the Minch from the ports of Back, Brevig, Coll and Tong." The cairn lists twelve disasters during the period from 1858 to 1922 which had claimed the lives of 79. It is also dedicated to all those from the area who had died at sea before 1851, when official death registration had began.

Beyond the Harbour I was able to continue along the cliff top until I picked up a track which lead back to the road at the northern end of Coll beach. Coll beach is a beautiful stretch of sand cupped in a wide bay. I had to rejoin the B895 road to cross the bridge over the River Coll but found a footway of sorts along the west side of the road. This took me past yet another, smaller, memorial to the land raiders of Coll. This celebrated the men who "took possession of Upper Coll in 1921, a town from which their ancestors had previously been evicted."

At the southern end of Coll beach I found a small park of mobile homes for holiday letting. Unexpectedly, because it was not shown on the map, I found that I was able to resume my cliff top walk adjacent to the caravan park. A track went past the caravans to the top of the cliff and there was, once again, enough space between the edge of the low cliff and the field fence. I found my way to the asphalt township road running through Tong. From the cliff top it is possible to admire a modern black house built in recent years to the design of the two Stephen brothers from Skye. They trade under the name Dualchas. Alasdair Stephen wrote a dissertation on the blackhouse which describes his inspiration, Werner Kissling, who worked in Eriskay in 1934.

I turned south west along the Tong township road. It ran straight and parallel to the coast before turning sharp west to join the B895. The road was quiet, deserted in fact but took me through a tranquil domestic scene. A man fixed the back wheel of his tractor at the road side. A little further along an old horse drawn plough lay in the ditch. The afternoon British Airways plane flew over-head on its way to Stornoway Airport just across the bay. I rejoined the main road and took the footway along the western side of the road to Tong Farm. Just before the farm the main road swept round a tight right hand bend and disappeared on its way to Stornoway. I walked down Ford Terrace, passed Tong Farm, went through a gate and walked down to the foreshore. The bay was full of water; alas I had missed the low tide so could not test the way across the sands. The lights of Stornoway gleamed across the water; tantalising.

My aim was to walk across Tong Sands to Stornoway as I believed that the route had been used until the 1950s. It is the shortest route from Tong to Stornoway, far shorter than the road. It seemed logical, therefore, that crofters drove their sheep and cattle across this ford on their way to market in Stornoway. However, there appeared to be no memory of this route and local officials advised against it on the grounds of safety. A route is shown on 1 inch OS maps which were current until well after the Second World War (the 'Popular' Sixth Edition). I knew the risks but de-cided to accept them with caution. I acknowledge that Mel-bost Sands, which lie seaward of Tong Sands beyond the sand spit Teanga Thung, are dangerous. Fast flowing tides at Melbost are capable of trapping the unwary. This might befall anyone not sticking to the old route across the Tong Sands.

After considerable homework I was ready to make the

crossing. I studied the tide tables published in the local paper, the *Stornoway Gazette*, and observed conditions on the sand. I planned to cross Tong Sands from Tong Farm to Culrigen on the outskirts of Stornoway exactly as shown on the 'Popular' edition of the OS maps. I advise all who follow me along this route to be careful. Take no unnecessary risks and accept that they cross at their own risk.

Despite all this preparation I remained nervous. The day of my crossing dawned. Despite my study of the tide tables I arrived at Tong a little early. I walked along Ford Terrace down to the foreshore to await low tide. Slowly but surely the sands emerged in the cold light of early morning. I passed the time reading a book. It was *For whom the bell tolls* by Ernest Hemingway. Ironically I came to the passage:

> So if your life trades its seventy years for seventy hours
> I have that value now and I am lucky enough to know
> it. And if there is not any such thing as a long time,
> nor the rest of your lives, nor from now on, but there
> is only now, why then now is the thing to praise and
> I am very happy with it.

I was not remotely facing death this morning but I knew there were risks. Tong Sands represented the unknown but it was also the moment when I was certain to be walking the old way.

I judged that the tide was finally out. 'Now' had come. It was a coldish grey morning. I did not feel heroic. Traffic passed safe along the road to Stornoway a way off beyond the saltings at the head of the bay. Many fears raced before my eyes; being lost in sinking sands, being drowned by a rapidly rising tide, getting lost on the sands and wandering out to sea. I reasoned that I would not loose my way if I could see Stornoway on the other side of the bay; I had my compass if fog clamped down. As for getting drowned, the tide was now out. It had gone out so slowly that it was difficult to believe that it would come in any more quickly. It would not come in unnoticed but I would be vigilant; the channels would fill first. I had no reason to doubt the stories of rapidly advancing tides. The rafts of saltings which formed the shore a few feet above the sands looked firm enough. They were high enough to keep me dry at high tide, low enough to scramble up if the tide came in very rapidly. The route marked on the map ran very close to this shore. I would be sensible, proceed with caution and go across without lingering.

I crossed the sands to the first channel of water. It was about eight metres wide. As I got closer I realised that the water was low enough to reveal a set of parallel wooden blocks about a foot apart jutting just above the water. Perhaps they once supported boards or maybe they were markers. Either way, there was little doubt that this was the place to cross. The blocks were as unexpected as the old marker posts on the moors. I crossed gingerly but the water did not rise above my ankles. A wide expanse of sand now stretched ahead. I walked in a straight line never more than ten metres from the low earth cliff which formed the shore. After all my anxieties I quickly picked up a line of tractor tyre marks stretching towards Stornoway. The sand here was a little slithery in places but it was firm. The OS Map marks this area "Sand and mud".

Stornoway was visible throughout my walk a distance of about 1½ miles. The place of my landfall was obscured by a headland. Once around it, the landfall was obvious. I could see that the track came down to the foreshore from a road

lined with houses and street lights. Before reaching it I had
to cross another water filled channel. This was about ten
metres wide and half a metre deep. There were makeshift
markers on the northern bank between which I made my
crossing. One looked like an old tyre, the other something
wrapped in plastic. I crossed, reached the foreshore and
eventually found myself in Sand Street. At the top of Sand
Street I turned left and walked into the centre of Stornoway.

Stornoway

Having found an acceptable route from the Butt to Stornoway I was optimistic about the rest of the walk through
Lewis and Harris, although some of the sections still presented a puzzle. I reckoned that my route of 32 miles from
the Butt could be walked comfortably in three days. Camping on the moor is possible in many places, Maoim or Upper Dibadale would be my choice because both have fresh
water. Another site might be the foreshore below Tong Farm
whilst waiting for the tide.

Stornoway's Local History Library is a rich and fascinating resource of books and archive materials with dedicated
and knowledgeable staff. I spent my soujourn checking the
finer points of my walk. It has always been a good place to
meet many of the islands' thinkers and historians.

Stornoway to Garenin

When the time came to leave Stornoway I walked along the
Quay in Cromwell Street the anchorage used by the local
fishing fleet and continued along the more prosaic pave-
ment in Cromwell Street. Traffic streamed past. I walked
across the footbridge over the Bayhead River and into the
tranquil grounds of Lewis Castle. The Bayhead River flows

down to the harbour and forms the boundary to the Castle grounds. The path to the bridge from Cromwell Street is adjacent to a green painted metal topped building used by local youth groups.

The Castle's picturesque grounds are public open space, another stipulation of Leverhulme's land gift. The Lews Castle College, part of the University of the Highlands and Islands, is housed in modern buildings in the centre of the Park. To the southern eye the Castle grounds provide familiar parkland landscape but this type of landscape is unusual for the islands which are largely treeless.

The 'castle' and the park were created in the nineteenth century by Sir James Matheson. Leverhulme continued its development. Matheson was no more popular than Leverhulme. He made his money from the opium trade with China but lived life in the islands according to the strict code of Victorian morals. A local author, Francis Thompson, highlighted Matheson's hypocrisy by quoting Disraeli who had dubbed him "McDrug".

My goal was to walk through the park to the A859, the Stornoway to Tarbert road, which forms the park's western boundary. There are two exits, the main gate and a laddered exit over the wall. The laddered exit is preceded by a board walk through woods. I chose to walk to the laddered exit as it took me closest to the junction with the A859. This was the basis of the route I planned to take to Carloway and Garenin.

My walk through the park was circuitous and yielded fine views of Tong Sands from one of the hills. The tide was out which allowed me to reflect with satisfaction on the route I had found from the Butt to Stornoway. Walking along the road from Tong to Stornoway looked unappealing compared to crossing the sands. I descended along

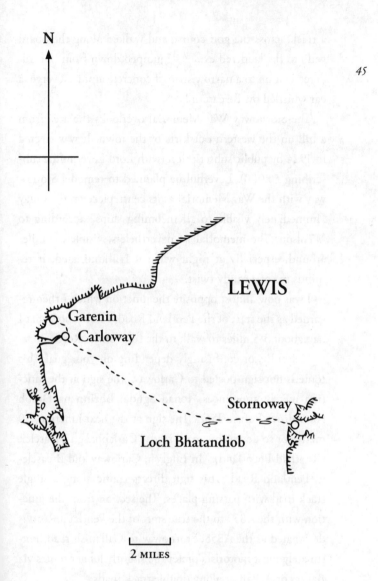

N

LEWIS

Garenin
Carloway

Stornoway

Loch Bhatandiob

2 MILES

Figure 4   Stornoway to Garenin

a track across the golf course and walked along the board walk to the laddered exit. As I jumped down from the laddered exit on to a narrow strip of concrete amidst a verge, a car whistled by. Be careful!

The Stornoway War Memorial overlooks the area from a hill on the western outskirts of the town. It was erected in 1924 by public subscription (with Lord Leverhulme subscribing £5,000). Leverhulme planned to remodel Stornoway with the War Memorial as its centrepiece on the Quay "immediately visible to all incoming ships" according to Nicolson. The memorial is, nevertheless, visible for miles around, especially at night when it is illuminated. It reminds me of a candy twist.

I was now almost opposite the junction which I then regarded as the start of the Pentland Road. I now know that I had about 3½ miles to walk to the start of the Road.

Helpfully, or confusingly depending on your goal, this route is not sign-posted to Carloway. The sign at the junction merely announces "Ionad Sgudal Bheinn na Drobh (Benadrove Refuse Tip)". The sign at the next junction, 50 metres or so down this road, reads "Carlabhavgh Breascleit (Rhathad Phentland)." In English, Carloway and Breascleit, Pentland Road. This sign directs traffic along a single track road with passing places. The section from the junction with the A859 to the true start of the Pentland Road is designated as the A858, Stornoway to Callanish road. Fortunately most motorists prefer the slightly longer routes via Barvas or Achamor along double track roads.

I continued along the road to the dump. A track beyond the dump lead to the true start of the Pentland Road. This seemed preferable to a single track road narrowed in places by fences. I had, however, not bargained for the heavy refuse trucks plying back and forth. After passing the houses I got

alongside Loch Airigh na Lic. The first summit yielded its reward – a glimpse of the hills of Uig and Harris to the south.
The asphalt road swept up on to the landfill site whilst the
way continued as a grass track beyond a gate. The landfill is
less of an eyesore than one might expect because it is partly
landscaped but I found the constant beeping from heavy
vehicles working the site intrusive. The landscaped area was
covered by a huge flock of mainly immature gulls.

As I walked along the track a wider view of the hills to
the south opened. Clisham, in Harris, (799 m) the highest
peak in the Outer Hebrides, was prominent nearly 25 miles
to the south. There were also glimpses of the hills of the
Uig area. The track was a little wet. I had to negotiate a gate
and clamber across a burn where a bridge had been demolished. The surrounding moor was interspersed by a number
of small pine plantations. Here and there I could see the
ruins of shielings. Some still stand alongside the A858 road
on the way to Callanish after it diverges from the start of
the Pentland Road.

The Pentland Road starts where the A858 to Callanish
(sign posted 'Acha Mòr' or 'Achamor') goes off to the south.
It runs some 16 miles to Carloway Pier with a branch to
East Loch Roag at Breasclete. Its whole route is now as-
phalted which makes for an easy walk, a luxury compared
to my earlier bog trotting on the Lewis Moor.

The road has an amusing history and is still shrouded
in some mystery. It was opened on 6 September 1912 by
Mr Mackinnon Wood, Secretary of State for Scotland. The
Marquis of Lothian, the first Secretary for Scotland to visit
the island, had suggested the idea some years earlier. He
saw the economic value of developing the natural harbours
at Breasclete and Carloway. A local committee was formed
to pursue the project but it favoured a railway rather than

a road, an option rejected by the Scottish Office. In 1893, after negotiations between the Scottish Office and the local committee, work started. It took sixteen years to complete. Work was delayed for some time after the first contractor went bankrupt and it was not until years later that another Secretary of State, John Sinclair, rescued the project. John Sinclair was Secretary of State for Scotland from 1905 to 1912, after which he was created Lord Pentland and became Governor of Madras, hence the name of the road.

I was intrigued to find the spot where the road was declared open. I scoured the area in the hope that there might be a stone or some other small memorial by the roadside. According to the *Highland News* of 14 September 1912 a ribbon was strung across the road at "Loch Fad and Eipe." It was cut by a pair of scissors from a box inscribed "Pentland Road, Stornoway to Carloway, opened 6 September 1912. Presented by Mr W J MacKenzie."

The name of the Loch did not appear on any contemporary map and meant nothing to any of my local friends. However, the first edition 6" map surveyed in 1852 gives the name of the loch close to the junction with the A858 as Airidh an Eipe. The second edition gives it as Vatandip. Current maps refer to the loch as Loch Bhatandiob. "Bh" in Gaelic is aspirated so could become "Fad". This lead me to conclude that the ceremony had taken place at or near the junction with the road to Callanish. Though I searched on both sides of the road I could find no sign of a memorial stone. Maybe the ribbon was simply held by men on either side of the road or strung between posts. But it did confirm that this point is the true beginning of the Pentland Road.

Ahead lay the west coast. I was keen to make progress and thanks to the Pentland Road I glided across the moor. The road climbs steadily upwards to a low pass. Beinn

Mhaol Stachaiseal (171 m) and Stacaseal (216 m) are to the north of this point. As I climbed to the pass a full panorama of the southern and western hills was revealed. I tried to identify them as I walked along. Of the Uig hills, the pointed hill Suainaval (429 m) stands proud of a double line of hills on either side of a valley. I identified Mealisval (574 m) with Tahaval (515 m) in the front row, Teinnasval (497 m) with Carcaval (514 m) behind and Tamanaisval (467 m) with Laival a Tuath (505 m) and Laival a Deas (501 m) behind. Closer, a portent of things to come, at the gates of the Morsgail estate, is Skeun (265 m) and Coduinn (241 m), with the three peaks Beinn a'Tuath, Beinn Mheadhonach (397 m) and Beinn a'Deas (351 m) behind. To the south but north of the Harris hills I believed I could see Scalabhal (260 m), a hill I would pass on my way to Kinlochresort.

What became apparent as I walked to the pass is that the route of the Pentland Road is levelled which lends credibility to the theory that the intention had been to build a railway. Today we take levelled roads for granted but plenty of island roads undulate across moor and mountain. A levelled route of this antiquity is unusual. Further credibility to the railway theory comes from the flat bed bridges which are crossed along its route and at Carloway the bridge which crosses the Pentland Road near its western end. One of these bridges, with a metal girder balustrade, is visible from the A859 on the outskirts of Stornoway. The bridge is on a now stranded tarmaced road which runs directly towards the town from the junction of the A858 and the road to the dump. The line continues north within the Castle grounds along an embankment towards Stornoway harbour.

Stornoway Local History library has a scale diagram showing the length of the road. Interestingly the diagram confirms that the route was intentionally levelled. This led me to speculate that the local committee agreed to go along with the Scottish Office's wish for a road, but worked to build a railway. A railway would have cost more than a road, so this may explain why the first contractor went bankrupt. It may also explain why the Scottish Office shelved the project for many years. Local rebellion was punished by official intransigence.

Some 6½ miles outside Stornoway I crossed the boundary of the Stornoway Parish and left the domain of the Stornoway Trust. I had been walking through Stornoway Parish since passing Loch Caol Duin Othail on the Lewis Moor, some 3 miles north of Tolsta.

Another issue interested me. Are there marker posts on this part of the moor? I asked two local friends and shepherds, Alec MacDonald, a local Councillor and Convenor of the Council from 1998 and D R Macleod, warden of the Gatliff Hostel at Garenin until 2002. Both confirmed that there are no markers on this part of the moor. If there were no artificial markers on the moor how did local shepherds gather their sheep in the autumn? D R told me that this is a communal effort. A line of men and dogs sweep south from the Bragar Hills to a fank near where the road crosses the River Creed. "You come over the top of the Bragar Hills and line yourself up with the TV mast on Eitseal, and you cannot go wrong" D R said. At least it is high enough not to loose line of sight in the bottom of some of the peat hags!

Some six miles from Carloway the road branches. One branch goes to Breasclete Pier, the other to Carloway. I continued towards Carloway through a landscape of hummocky hills and rocky crags and passed lochs with wooded islands in deep hollows in the moor. As I got closer to Carloway the landscape became rockier. The road picks up the course of the Carloway River and runs alongside it from Loch Laxavat Lorach to Carloway Pier. Shortly after I passed the waterworks, some council houses and continued to Carloway bridge. High above is Carloway Free Church. Unusually for island churches, its gable is complete with a bell.

I walked under the A858 Barvas to Callanish road and climbed up the far side of the embankment and turned towards Garenin. As I walked the final 1½ miles along the undulating road to the old village of Garenin the thatched roofs of the village became visible on the coast. In the village, past the gate and the village entrance sign, the Hostel is the first thatched building on the right.

I was glad to get to the Hostel. It had been a long day. It was an 18½ mile walk from Stornoway, most of it against the oncoming wind. My face glowed. I sank down in an armchair and enjoyed the warmth of the fire. Someone gave me a cup of tea. Bliss.

Chapter 4

GARENIN, CALLANISH AND
THE WEST SIDE

GARENIN WAS THE last Lewis village of inhabited black houses. It is now a village of restored black houses. Abandoned in 1974 its last residents lived in number 5, the house which is now the Hostel. It became a Conservation Area at about this time and from 1991, when the Hostel opened, the renovation of the village has been the responsibility of the Garenin Trust (Urras nan Geàrrannan). It was officially opened by the Princess Royal in 2001 and is now a superb tourist attraction. Jim Crawford, with the help of his son and his wife, thatched the village buildings. They stand as yet another example of Jim's artistic contribution to the landscape of the islands.

The village provides accommodation for different tastes. As well as the Youth Hostel it also includes luxury holiday cottages. There is a cafe, a reconstructed historic blackhouse, interpretative facilities and a study room which can be used by visiting school, university and youth groups.

Aerial views show that the preserved village is but a vestige of a larger village. Most of the newer houses along the road from Uraghag to the village stand adjacent to ruined black houses. Indeed aerial views of most of the villages of the west side of Lewis show this pattern. Typically families have built their new homes alongside their old homes.

Beyond the village the track winds down to a shingle bay. A way-marked walk has been laid out to Dalmore Bay. The current is too dangerous for swimming in Garenin Bay but Dalmore is safe, if you can stand the cold water.

The Lewis black house, as a type, is long and narrow with a double stone wall, the cavity filled with puddled clay and peat. The thatch is traditionally domed, overlaps the wall head, and is roped down with an elaborate lattice design weighed down by rocks. One end of the building was used as a byre for the cattle, the other end a dwelling. Many of the Garenin houses have flat stones protruding from the walls to provide access to the roof. The Black House at Arnol, a few miles north of Garenin, is a good example of the condition of these houses in the nineteenth century. This house is in the care of Historic Scotland.

The Gatliff Trust, of which I am a trustee, commented in its triennial report for 1982-1984, "Until very recently, while the crofter had protected rights of tenure and could build and use houses for himself and family, he could not sell them if he decided to move elsewhere or build the modern house he preferred." This was because house and croft were a single legal entity. "Vacant houses, " the Gatliff Trust continued, "were thus left empty to fall into disrepair, or to be used as byres or stores ... We believe these changed circumstances should cause the public authorities to re-examine their policies on how to preserve thatched cottages ... These house are an asset to the local tourist trade, and an important part of the heritage of the Outer Hebrides; a number are worthy of preservation."

The policy has shifted in favour of conservation and Garenin is one result, but the cost has been phenomenal, culminating in a £1.2 million Millennium scheme to com-

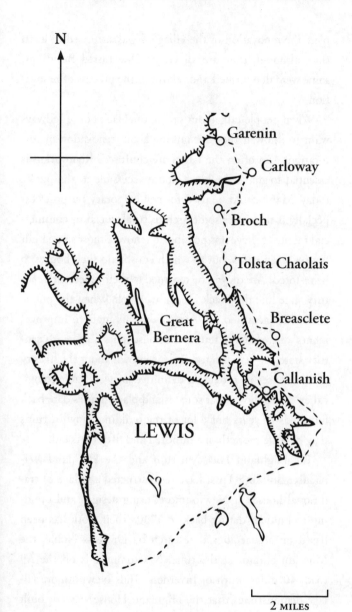

Figure 5   Garenin to Morsgail

plete the renovation of the village. I was surprised to learn that, although they are all Grade One Listed Buildings, some were demolished and rebuilt in the process of renovation.

When people talk about saving the black house I always want to know if they are talking about renovation or restoration. Too often the issues are confused. Renovation is essential to make the black house accessible to the public today. Many could be used for contemporary purposes especially if they offer some architectural, social or commercial merit. I believe it is possible to renovate most stone built houses, even ruins, but to which era should such houses to be restored? Are they to be returned to their nineteenth century state like the Black House at Arnol? When the public authorities acquired the Arnol house its modern improvements were erased to return the house to its nineteenth century state. At Garenin too little is known about the history of the houses to provide a definitive answer. Archaeological evidence shows that some island black houses date back hundreds of years but a lot of the buildings now in ruins may be little more than a hundred and fifty years old.

The Highland Folk Museum and the Highland Vernacular Building Trust have reconstructed a village of traditional houses at Newtonmore, using designs and building techniques dating back to 1700. Their work has been based on archaeological research by Dr Ross Noble, the Museum curator at the time. Newtonmore is on the A9 road, 40 miles south of Inverness. Thus Newtonmore village demonstrates that the Highland House was not built as a permanent dwelling. It was built round a wooden cruck frame that could be taken apart and re-erected elsewhere. The walls were made of woven wooden mats constructed from local wood, resting on a low stone foundation. Turfs were piled against the mat walls for insulation. The roof was tiled in turf and covered in heather (or some other material such as bracken) pulled up, not cut, from the local moor. Building was a vernacular skill developed from experience and perfected by the constant attention required to maintain such buildings. Thatching material varied according to that which was available locally. A wide range of material is on display at Newtonmore.

In contrast to the Highland house, stone was used in the Hebridean house because there was so little wood in the islands. Nevertheless, it was still a temporary dwelling to be vacated, until 1886, at the end of the lease on the land (typically twenty years) or at the whim of the landlord. When the family moved the roof would be removed and the cruck frame timbers taken to a new location. All the other materials would be left in situ, perhaps to be reused by incoming tenants, but largely because they were readily available in the new location. This leads me to wonder if the tumbled down roofs we see today are the first permanent roofs erected on the walls.

If this is so it seems misguided to define too tightly materials and methods that may be used today to renovate thatched houses. (Restoration for historical reference is a different matter.) If materials are to hand locally they should be used. Traditional island roofs were made of marram bent laid on turfs, but heather was also used. It is not uncommon to find driftwood and broken oars used in roof construction. Today imported wood is readily available and it is logical for renovations to use boarded roofs. Felt laid on top of timber provides a waterproof base for the thatch, laid, perhaps on a harness of chicken wire. These methods have been used at Garenin, and at Berneray Hostel (since 1985) and elsewhere in the islands. Howmore Hostel, however, has been renovated using traditional turfs on timbers instead of a boarded roof.

My day at Garenin was driech. In the calm of the Hostel common room I reflected on the history of this house. Its age is not known but it was "modernised" and extended in the 1920s. (Was this when it acquired its distinctive gable end with sash window?) It was the home of Duncan MacLeod, who was born in the house, his wife who came from Shawbost, and their daughters, Annie, Peggy and Christy. In his youth Duncan had been a seaman but later he worked the land of this croft entirely by hand. He kept hens and cows, grew oats, barley and potatoes.

His daughters were fisher girls who followed the herring-fishing along the east coast of Britain as far south as Lowestoft. They formed a "crew" in which Christy and Annie gutted the fish whilst Peggy packed them into barrels. The fishing ended in 1939, when they came home to weave Harris Tweed. Christy filled the bobbins while her sisters wove. The loom was housed in the outhouse opposite, which was also used to house the hens. The outhouse is now the village study room.

As the sisters grew older they contented themselves on the croft giving hospitality to the many people from all over the world who came to visit this unique village. In 1965 Christy died and about seven years later so did Peggy but Annie lived in the house for another year until she fell and broke her hip. After her return from hospital she lived with a kind lady in Dalbeg for a few years but ended her days in hospital in 1985 aged ninety-three.

As the day ended I sat on the stones piled on the beach and considered my route south. My goal was the deserted village of Kinlochresort which stood at the head of the sea loch Loch Resort in the heart of Morsgail Forest. It was miles from the nearest road. Herbert Gatliff had first talked to me about Kinlochresort in 1975. I wanted my route from Garenin to Kinlochresort to include the Carloway Broch and the Callanish Stones. These sites showed that the history of human occupation of the islands went back many thousands of years. Little is recorded of that history. Then, like now, island society was dominated by an oral tradition.

The first part of my route would not be difficult as an old road ran over the moor from Carloway towards Breasclete. However the southern part of its route had been overlain by the asphalt road, the A858 from Carloway to Callanish, much of which is single track with no footway. After my experience on the way from Tolsta to Tong I was confident that I would find an alternative. Although the A858 was the principle route south I felt sure that there must have been subsidiary tracks and paths used to walk from house to house. I had studied local maps and aerial photos and some possible routes had emerged.

The following morning I returned to Carloway Bridge along the undulating road from Garenin and turned south along the A858 road out of Carloway past the police station. Shortly afterwards the road took me back on to the moors with its rocky crags. I found the start of the old road at a five barred gate. The Carloway History Society in its pamphlet *Country Walk* says the old road is a "grassy path … once the main road that linked Carloway with Tolsta Chaolais, Breasclete and Callanish. The current road was completed in the mid 1800s but for a long time afterwards people used the old road as it was the shorter route."

The way was about ten feet wide, slightly higher and greener than its surroundings which were generally rocky hills. Patches of heather grew in places. Most of the culverts under the road had collapsed but the resulting ruts did not present a major obstacle. A fence cut the route but I was able to cross it without difficulty and continued round the top of a loch. I climbed higher through a pass. The top of the rise brought views over the island of Great Bernera and the hills around Uig beyond the local hills. After a bend, the path continued to the south east towards Breasclete but I wanted to visit the Broch and carried on in a westerly direction across the rocky moor. I passed through a low dip in the ridge flanked by craggy outcrops and walked to the brow. The road was about 100 foot below. I could see how to scramble down. The Carloway History Society's book re-assured me that I would find a gate below in the fence at the roadside.

The brow of the ridge gave a fine view of the Broch and the disused 'lazy beds' in the field opposite. Lazy beds are inappropriately named ridges of heaped up soil often in wide parallel strips, used for growing vegetables and per-haps other crops. I have never understood why they were called 'lazy' – working the beds must have been hard work. It was a tricky climb down the steep slope to the road but I found the gate and walked back along the A858 to the turn which took me to the road to the Broch and its Interpreta-tion Centre.

The Broch is atmospheric. Its origins and age are un-known but it is assumed to be Iron Age. However, it was used by successive generations of peoples for hundreds of years. Its bottle shaped concentric stone walls are sliced open to the north and rise to a point. The Broch appears to have been used as a defensive home, a fortress and a potter's workshop. Ian Armit believes it was still used for defensive reasons in the sixteenth century during conflicts between neighbouring clans.

The Broch fascinated me. It was worth the short detour but now I had to return to the task of finding a route south. Mark Chamberlain found a walk from the Broch to Tolsta Chaolais. This is listed in his book of *Walks from Garenin Hostel*. He suggests continuing west along the road from the Broch to the end of Loch an Dùin and then going south around the western shore of Loch Honagro. I was tempted to use this route but I wanted to pass the Doune Braes Hotel as this would take me to the old road to Tolsta Chaolais.

The 1:50000 map showed a short track going south parallel to the A858. I walked back towards the A858 and turned down south down a short asphalt road just before the junction with the A858. This route continued more directly south alongside a fence built on a residual stone wall. The wall was built on a mound perhaps originally a turf and stone wall, a traditional design once common in the islands. The fence and wall fringed the face of a steep but low hill, part of the area's common grazings. I reached the rear of the Doune Braes Hotel on the shore of Loch an Dunain.

The Doune Braes Hotel was once a school and the old road from Tolsta Chaolais to the hotel was built for children to get to school. Nineteenth century legislation required children to attend schools so the Congested Districts Board, set up in 1897, funded the construction of footpaths. This continued until the start of the First World War. After the War the County Councils took responsibility for the funding. (I guess today's school children prefer the bus.) At that time Lewis and Harris fell under Ross-shire County Council, whilst Uist and Barra were under Inverness-shire.

The old road begins in front of the hotel and goes over the hill to Tolsta Chaolais. It affords good views of the Loch and its dun. After the brow there is a good view of the Harris hills to the south. A dun, most often found on an island, is a small fortified tower erected for defensive purposes. The islands' lochs are dotted with duns. Most are now just piles of stones. From the brow the old road took me down to Tolsta Chaolais. I joined the road into the village after crossing a well made stone slab bridge. Tolsta Chaolais is a pretty village, quiet and hidden away from the A858. The more southerly part of the village is on the shore of Loch à Bhaile from which a burn runs the short distance to the sea in a deep valley. As the road leaves the village to return to the A858 it bends inland and crosses the valley on an embankment. As I rounded the turn I thought I could see the track to Breasclete which I had seen on the 1854 map and on aerial photographs. It was running south from the eastern side of the burn.

I clambered down the embankment and joined the track. Initially it was well defined and went over a rocky hill to another valley. The valley revealed another thrill: a small ruined mill, complete with millstone where the path crossed the burn. It reminded me of the restored mill at Shawbost, another building restored and thatched by Jim Crawford.

Beyond the mill the track climbed to a large craggy knoll and went along a noticeable ledge above the shore of the sea loch East Loch Roag. This took me to a five barred metal gate after which the track disappeared. The line of the 1854 route suggested a compass bearing of 150°. Using this bearing I found myself crossing a high open moor fringed on the west by cliffs. There was little evidence of the route across the moor but continuing on the 150° bearing I came across a seven foot high post exactly on the 1854 route. It seemed to mark a safe place to cross a stream in the middle of a rather boggy area.

From this point the 1854 track went directly to a house which I could see a short distance away. Aerial photographs

taken in 1946 as part of the survey of Scotland confirmed
this and showed that at the time this house was thatched.
Now it is modernised with a slate roof and enclosed on a
fenced plot. A five barred gate gave access to the front of
the house. I skirted the feu and took the new track from
the front of the house to the A858. I suspected that the
1854 track joined the road to Breasclete by taking the shortest route. Today this would mean crossing several fences.
It hardly seemed worth it as I could reach the road down
the drive to the house. Walking along the A858 was not so
bad. A footway started after a short distance and took me
to the end of the road which looped through Breasclete village. I guessed this loop was the old road which had been
by-passed in more recent times by the modern A858. The
village stands on the side of a hill. As the loop took me
higher it opened a wonderful panorama of North Harris
and Clisham to the south and to the west the hills of the
Uig area across East Loch Roag.

Breasclete impressed me as a charming township, a mixture of old stone houses and modernised houses in diverse
styles including tiny old houses made of wooden boards.
Most of these were used as byres. In the year 2000 Breasclete Park won the Crofting township Award (give by the
Scottish Crofters Union and Scottish Natural Heritage) for
their "co-operative endeavours and environmentally sensi-
tive crofting". No wonder I had been impressed.

The loop was crossed by the spur from the Pentland Road
on its way to Breasclete Pier. At the Pier I could see the three
red towers of a factory making perfumes from fish oils. It
was built in the style of an Italian hill village to a design of
Stuart Bagshaw and Matt Bruce.

Breasclete Primary school was at the southern junction
of the loop with the main road. It had been one of the first

schools to use Gaelic medium teaching. Opposite the junction is the derelict Breasclete Mill, a large two storey industrial building more like Gress Mill than the older, smaller, Shawbost or Tolsta Chaolais Mills.

From here a footway goes west to within 100 metres of the turn to Callanish. When it disappeared I walked along the verge. As I walked along the A858 the Callanish Stones came into view on their hill at the southern end of Callanish village. I turned off the A858 and walked to the Stones past an upturned boat in a farm yard and the black house tea room, which is the last house before the stones.

The Callanish Stones have a cruciform pattern with a central circle. The 53 stones were re-erected in the nineteenth century. Sir James Matheson had them removed from the peat. There are thought to be up to twelve other megalithic sites in the area associated with the Callanish Stones, some of which are stone circles. I was due to pass one shortly after leaving Callanish.

There is a modern Visitor Centre just down the hill and out of sight from the Stones. I paused for tea and soup. I had walked 11¼ miles from Garenin Hostel to Callanish. To reach the gates of the Morsgail estate I had to walk a further 11½ miles.

I could see no alternative to continuing along the A858 and then the B8011 south. Morsgail was the key to Kinlochresort and the shortest route to Bo'glas in Harris. Kinlochresort could also be reached from the Uig area but this represented a long detour on foot.

I resumed my journey via the car park outside the Visitor Centre. A party of school children on a school trip laughed and joked with one another as they mingled with the tourists disembarking from coaches or cars. I walked to the A858 and turned south. I found that the road was flanked by a reasonable verge and vestiges of the old road. From the Tigh Melross restaurant (renowned for its cuisine) I was able to use a footway to the junction with the B8011 at Garynahine. At the turn I changed maps from OS 1:50000 sheet 8 to sheet 13. The turn also represented the moment when I finally left behind the influence of the Lewis Moor. Garynahine was also the last settlement I would encounter until I got to Bo'glas in Harris.

The B8011 is a recently upgraded and straightened road which crosses a rocky wilderness. The area is dotted with lochs, small and large, and dominated to the south by the triple peaks of Beinn a'Chuailein, Beinn a'Sgurran and Ben Mohal. Caultrashal Beag at the end of Little Loch Roag provides a focus for the walk after the Great Bernera turn. Beyond is the much higher massif of Beinn Mheadgabach rising to over 397 metres.

From the turn at Garynahine I walked down the B8011 to a bridge. Walking along the new road was acceptable, it was not busy but the infrequent traffic passed at speed. It had a good verge on both sides. Just beyond this bridge I found my first piece of old road. This ran for about 100 metres before rejoining the new road. After the turning to Great Bernera, about three miles from Garynahine, I found the old road was intact for over 8 miles. The only obstacle was a burn in a narrow valley about 10 metres deep. The bridge across the valley had been demolished, it was said, to ease passage for the salmon. The burn was not full of water so I managed to scramble up and down the valley side. The Council still owns the way-leaves along this old road. Camping is possible in a number of quiet spots.

Shortly before the Bernera turn, a fisherman's track went south west along the side of Abhainn Grimersta. I had toyed with the idea of using this track as part of the route but an acquaintance argued against. He had spent a university summer holiday as a fish watcher on this complex of lochs during which time he lived in a wooden hut down this track.

Despite my foreboding at Garynahine about using the B8011 I had got to the gates of the Morsgail after a pleasant, easy walk, undisturbed by traffic. I was keen to start my walk across the Morsgail Forest at the beginning of a day, so called a halt when I got to the southern end of Little Loch Roag, near the gates to Morsgail.

Chapter 5

KINLOCHRESORT

IN MY MINDS-EYE Kinlochresort had always been an icon of the Hebridean wilderness. Not surprisingly, it was a key goal of my walk. It also lay on the shortest route between Callanish and Rhenigidale.

Kinlochresort is a deserted village of a few houses on a remote sea loch on the border between Harris and Lewis miles from any road. The village had been inhabited until about 1965.

It was said to be a beautiful place, with fine views over the hills of North Harris and especially of Sròn Ulladale a cliff overhang amidst those hills. There was a time when every other German backpacker I met in North West Scotland wanted to visit Sròn Ulladale as it was mentioned Martin Velbinger's guide, *Schottland*. (It was dropped from later editions.)

A route across Morsgail Forest to Kinlochresort was marked on the 1899 and 1964 editions of 6" maps but the track which appears on contemporary 1:50000 maps veers off more directly south and does not reach Kinlochresort. After my experience on the Lewis Moor I made no assumptions about how I would find my way to the village across the moor.

In 1992 the *West Highland Free Press* suggested that the route may be blocked by a hostile estate. This suggestion came in an account of a walk to Kinlochresort by Ian Mitchell, a former teacher, now a freelance writer (not the Ian Mitchell who wrote the controversial book *Isle of the West*). Mitchell reported that the moor was impossible to navigate. He got lost on his way back from Kinlochresort and had walked to the shores of Loch Langavat. He said that the estate was owned by "an Englishman" and implied that he did not like visitors. Because of this, the way to Kinlochresort may be blocked. Brian Wilson, then the paper's publisher added a postscript to the article, "Ian Mitchell is right to focus upon an area of great beauty, which once sustained people, but is now incorporated entirely into an absentee owned estate." Brian Wilson became an MP in 1987 and from 1997 held a string of Ministerial Offices, including spells at both the Scottish and Scotland Offices.

I put these points to Simon Fraser, the estate's Factor. He said Ian Mitchell was incorrect. Walkers were welcome so long as they did not disturb the stalking or fishing or walk past the Lodge. Simon Fraser served as Chairman of the North West Area Board of Scottish Natural Heritage, the Government agency which holds the ring in Scotland on the access debate. (The "Englishman" died in 2004.)

It was Herbert Gatliff who had fired my imagination about Kinlochresort. Gatliff, (1897 to 1977) founded the Gatliff Trust in 1961, after he retired from the Civil Service, to perpetuate his interests in youth hostels and the outdoor movement. For most of his adult life Herbert supported an eclectic range of outdoor, amenity and other causes. He wanted young people to take control of their destiny, have their say in the way organisations are run, visit wild, untouched and remote places and record them in words, pic-

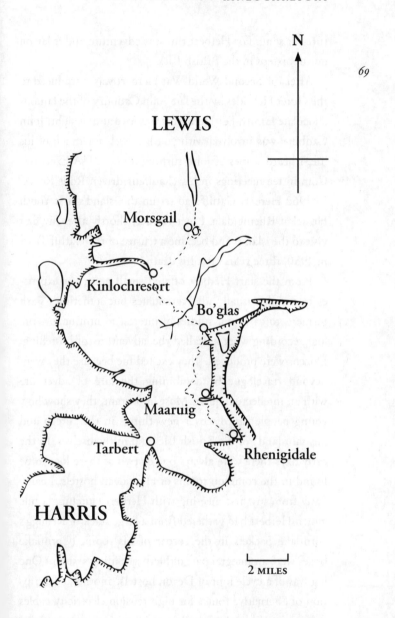

Figure 6 Morsgail to Kinlochresort and on to Rhenigidale

tures or song. For Herbert this was adventure and it lay on our doorsteps in the British Isles.

After the Second World War Herbert was introduced to the Outer Hebrides by the late John Cadbury of the famous chocolate family. For Herbert it was love at first sight. John Cadbury was involved with youth hostels for much of his life. I heard stories of John turning up for YHA Executive Committee meetings in his chauffeur driven Rolls Royce. In 1962 Herbert Gatliff had set up the island's first Youth Hostel at Rhenigidale. I met Herbert shortly after my first visit to the islands and became a trustee of the Gatliff Trust in 1980, three years after his death.

From the start Herbert offered small grants or expenses to people, usually undergraduates but sometimes sixth formers, to carry out studies of interest to him or to write logs recording what he called the 'adventure' of hostelling. Dozens were produced. They excited me because they went beyond travelogue by combining the lure of adventure with an intellectual quest. Most important, they show how young people can discover new things in the "green and pleasant land" of the British Isles and in themselves. In the early days there were always one or two of these logs to be found in the common rooms of Hebridean hostels. I came away from my first meeting with Herbert clutching a pile which Herbert had gathered from a large stack of Kellogg's cornflake packets in the corner of his room. (Cornflake boxes were an integral part of Herbert's filing system.) One log was of a cycle tour of Devon hostels, another a description of alternative routes for high tension electricity cables from the mainland to the Isle of Skye. A third was about central Wales, an area called the Elineth. Earlier in 1975 I had purchased a YHA pamphlet on the Elineth to guide me on a visit I made in August that year. I was not surprised to learn that Herbert had been behind its production. Herbert inspired me to realise that much of the British Isles is off the beaten track, remains unknown and is waiting to be re-discovered by each new generation, this generation no less than my own. The Gatliff logs inspire. They encourage us to take a fresh look at our own land, our home, our place. The quests in Britain logged by Gatliff's disciples in the 1960s and 1970s deepen our understanding of this country and, indirectly, of our self perception. Today Britain is off the beaten track for too many. It is not the destination of choice. It is far from chic in the popular eye. More often it is seen as a predictable, known, familiar and therefore dull land. Worse, many regard it as dank, chilly and forbidding. These logs present a view of Britain as a place where adventure is still possible especially in places like Kinlochresort.

Herbert was fascinated by Kinlochresort and it had been mentioned in several logs. Some months after my first visit to Kinlochresort I read David Stones' 1965 footpath and landscape survey in the Hebrides and the North West Highlands. These can be found in Herbert's papers which are held in the Bodleian Library in Oxford (as can an example of his Cornflake box storage system). Stone had visited Kinlochresort at Herbert's request to investigate the idea of the Trust starting a hostel in the village. By the time Stone arrived the residents had left rendering the idea impractical. Stone recorded:

> KINLOCHRESORT – the head of Loch Resort (pronounced ray-zort), obviously; but where is Loch Resort – that's perhaps not such an easy one. If the name does not ring a bell it is hardly surprising, for this sea loch is one of Britain's remotest, tucked away as it is on the west coast of the Outer Hebrides, right

on the Harris-Lewis county boundary. Here is a corner of Scotland that is little known and even less visited; the terrain is rough, places of accommodation are few and far between, and a footpath is a luxury; not an inviting prospect for the average tourist – but walkers' territory par excellence. Kinlochresort itself is set in the middle of an enormous bog which extends for at least a mile in every direction; beyond this to the south are the Harris hills, to the north the Uig hills, to the east the low hills flanking the west short of Loch Langaghat, and to the west, of course the sea.

In a subsequent log on *Landscape problems in the North West Highland* Herbert had commented:

The problem (at Kinlochresort) is not one of possible change, but of access ... I have been told however that the track passed Kinlochresort is the old right of way between West Lewis and West Harris, and walkers are therefore free to use it and in view of its length stop for rest on the way, though it is of course good manners in the stalking season to let the local people know in case they are going to be out on the hills. While the use of the route is never likely to be great, it is of quite considerable value to those who are prepared to make the effort to walk it, indeed I would go so far as to say one of the most important 'access' routes in Britain. A shelter at Kinlochresort is not essential for access, but if it could be made available by one or other of the estates would increase the value of the route, and incidentally bring its use a bit more under control.

Kinlochresort maintained its fascination for Herbert Gatliff. In September 1968 he encouraged another student, Chris Wright, to visit the area. Wright said of one of the evenings he spent at Kinlochresort:

> It was a lovely still evening and I sat out in the sun on the short cropped grass in front of the cottage, and after dinner I slept in the adjoining barn. This place was truly a haven of peace, the splash of the peaty burns and leaping salmon the only sounds to disturb the evening twilight, then the cones of Sròn Ulladale and Sròn Scourst merging with the clouds of a gathering night.

The day of my first visit to Kinlochresort (in 1998) was one of high expectation. I started at the gates of Morsgail Estate. The spot had a strangely unwelcoming air which made me feel nervous. It was bristling with forbidding notices. I hoped they were not intended to distract the determined walker. A prominent sign declared "Morsgail Lodge Private Road". Another, "No Parking" in red letters on a white background. A little beyond the gate was first the sign "No dogs" in red then a sign rendered illegible by age on which only one letter remained.

The Morsgail Estate had been one of the areas sub-divided for sale after Leverhulme's death. It is principally an area of moor, mountain and loch used for sport, in other words hunting and fishing. This use of the word 'estate' should not be confused with its use as the description of an area of suburban housing or an area of land laid out with smallholdings.

The map showed a track running into the estate from the gate but it was overgrown. The estate road went down the valley of a fast flowing river surrounded by low hills. The view was restricted by bends. One was wooded with rhodo-dendron and fir trees. This sense of enclosure increased my feeling of insecurity. The river was well looked after with artificial weirs for trout or salmon fishing. I continued my solitary progress expecting shouts or shots to ring out bring-ing my dream of a short route to Kinlochresort to an end, but none came.

When the Lodge came into sight, I was disappointed that it was so small. It looked like a 1960s suburban house with a steeply pitched roof, white walls and a creeper grow-ing up one end. I learned later that the original lodge was destroyed by fire. There were no vehicles at the house which suggested that no-one was at home.

As I got closer to the house I came upon a notice with an arrow. It read "Private. Walkers this way". I laughed out loud. After all the prohibitive notices at the gate walkers were now politely asked to go to the left across a neat bridge, rather than straight ahead to avoid passing directly in front of the house. Nearby I saw a bird scarer, one of those auto-matic firing mechanism with a red funnel. I wondered if it was used to deter unwanted walkers. I was more than happy to follow the arrow on the notice and crossed the river by a well made wooden bridge with no handrails. On the other side was a shed with a canvas roof which housed a six wheel motorised bog buggy.

The route took me around the east side of Loch Morsgail. It began to pelt with rain. I quickly donned my over-trousers and tightened my jacket and rucksack. I caught a glimpse of unsightly patches of car tyres laid to bridge the boggier stretches for the six wheeled vehicle. At the end of the loch I went through an old metal gate in the fence and continued around the southern shore. I crossed a narrow bridge with a hand rail over the Abhainn a' Lòin, a river feeding the Loch. From here I picked up the track south which ran from the lodge on to the moor. According to the map it would take me to another bridge back across the Abhainn a' Lòin from which the track ran towards Kinlochresort.

The ground was water logged but there were stones in the boggier spots. The track quickly narrowed and thanks to the rain, was running with water. A stiff southerly breeze blew up but thankfully the wind was not cold. I continued with my head down, beleaguered by the driving rain and beguiled by the track, both of which discouraged me from looking at the map. When I came to a bend in the river without passing the bridge shown on the map I realised I was off course. I returned along the river bank and found the bridge supports lying in the river bed. The bridge no longer existed.

I chose my crossing point with care. The river ran across boulders, was full and was about five metres wide. If it had been in spate I would have had no alternative but to return to the footbridge near the loch and take the southern bank. The southern bank looked soggy. I walked up and down the northern bank before choosing a spot to cross. The site of the former bridge looked best. There is nothing worse than walking with wet boots and socks. It is also difficult to cross rock strewn rivers in bare feet. The water is usually cold and the rocks can cut your feet. I carry a pair of old laced canvas shoes for use in hostels. I put these on and crossed without incident.

On the southern bank I dried my feet as best I could and replaced my boots and socks. My sodden plimsolls hung on to the back of my rucksack as I continued south. From the 'bridge' there was a good wide track going south as far as I could see in the mist and rain. I passed a junction marked with a stick but continued more directly south on the better path. Shortly after the junction the map showed a spot marked 'shieling'. The 1899 and 1964 maps showed this as the point of departure for the route or track to Kinlochresort. After seeing shielings on the Lewis Moor I expected an old dwelling like those I had seen at Maoim and Dibadale but I was in for another surprise.

I found that this 'shieling' was three bee-hive houses. The roof of the central house was intact and inhabited by a jenny wren. It gave me a "chirp" of welcome. I climbed inside through the low entrance door to shelter from the rain. The space was big enough to allow me to stand almost upright. The stones kept off a lot of the rain, so I sat down and had a cup of coffee from my flask. It had taken me an hour to reach this spot from the estate gates.

This was my first encounter with beehive houses though I had read a lot about them. In design a beehive house looks like a stone igloo with stones piled in decreasing concentric circles eventually meeting at the top. This style is said to use Neolithic building technology. I guess that some turfs might have been applied to part or all of the structure to make it wind and rain proof.

Histories of the islands written by W Anderson Smith and Geddes illustrate a large beehive house demolished in 1992. Jim Crawford told me that this had stood close to the turn to Uig from the A858 at Garynahine. He believes that small beehives, such as this on the way to Kinlochresort, were built as retreats by religious men on pilgrimage. In other words they were homes for hermits. But they seemed too small to allow anyone to lie down to sleep. According to the Highland Folk Museum this was not an issue. It was common practice in the Highlands for people to sleep sitting upright as lying down was regarded as the posture of the dead. Jim Crawford thinks it likely that up to three men would huddle together in a beehive hut for warmth.

After the rain eased I made ready for my onward journey. The 'shieling' stood on the banks of a burn. On its southern bank was a low hill. The track to the south crossed the burn at a plank bridge of gnarled wood and continued up the hill. I assumed this was the track which missed Kinlochresort. To the west was a second bridge across the burn made of six telegraph poles in two bands of three with two iron posts either side to mark its entrance. The line I had drawn on my map from the 1899 and 1964 maps gave a bearing of 220° from the 'shieling'. The track south was not on that alignment, but the bridge to the west was closer.

The telegraph pole bridge was slippery but I survived it. I took a bearing of 220° on my compass and set off across the trackless moor. The moor to the south was undulating. The ridges and troughs were covered by wispy grass and were more pronounced than on the Lewis Moor. I quickly realised I was south of the 1899 and 1964 line as I was not encountering the right pattern of lochans. I climbed to the top of a ridge for a better view. The correct route was not readily apparent. I reasoned that so long as I kept to 220° I would come to the shore of Loch Resort and could then walk along it to the village.

Loch Leatha came into view to the west. A couple of hooded crows were blown sky-ward by the wind. They were the first living things I had seen since leaving the estate gates. This struck me as odd, as I would have expected to see sheep.

The spurs marking the three glens to the south of Kinlochresort were now clear but the glens themselves were full of mist. It was easy to keep the bearing on Glen Ulladale. A line of posts appeared, some broken down. Were they the remains of a line of telegraph poles? The bases looked like broken down tree trunks but in one or two places the remains of the pole lays rotting alongside the stump. I wondered if this represented the 1899/1964 route. A grouse flew past.

I followed the line of posts but quickly realised this could not have been the route. It was impossible to walk along their line as it crossed small lochans surrounded by soggy ground. Shortly afterwards Loch Resort came into view. I saw the first house in Kinlochresort. It was white fronted with a blue door. Then I saw two isolated houses, one with a rusty red roof on the other side of the bay. A third house with a slate roof, patched at one end with a large section of corrugated iron came into view. Two or three sheep were dotted about. Seagulls wheeled above. An inflatable boat with an outboard motor was moored close to the southern shore of the Loch. The house with the blue door looked as if it was in occasional use, I guessed by game keepers. A large red calor bottle stood at the door and a blue pipe came down the slope from the River Housar, I assumed to provide a pressurised water supply.

I was about half a mile off course, so had to make my way along the northern shore of the Loch. This misalignment had not been too serious as I was soon able to pick up a well made track which lead me through empty stone gate posts in the field boundary to a house on the northern side of the Loch.

Loch Resort is a fjord, a sea loch stretching some six miles inland from the Atlantic. The island of Scarp loomed at the mouth of the loch. There had been a Gatliff Hostel on Scarp from 1965 to 1971. It had been found by Frank Martin. Frank had become the Chair of the Gatliff Trust on Herbert's death in 1977. Recent books about the island by

Angus Duncan and Calum J MacKay mention the Hostel.

The village was silent, tranquil with great presence, all of which made it beautiful in a gentle way. It was all, and more, that I had expected. I stopped to take in this moment.

Although I was referring to Kinlochresort, Ian Mitchell points out that the village is divided between Luachair to the south and Crola to the north. I had arrived at Crola where only one house stood. It looked in good condition but was sealed, its lower windows filled with stones. One of the upper windows was blocked with corrugated iron, the other with corrugated perspex. It had lost its rhones. An 'H' shaped pottery chimney sat on one chimney stack. An old stone byre stood next to the house. Its roof had fallen in. To the west of the house the wall of the house's enclosure curled around a huge pink-grey rock. A small tree grew in the rocks of the ridge on which the house was built. Some Ballachulish slates were piled up against the wall; obviously a supply for winter repairs. Behind the house was a terrace supported by a well made stone wall. Six narrow steps up the middle of the wall gave access to the top of the terrace.

The village is divided by a fast deep river, the Abhainn Mhòr Cearn Resort flowing from Glen Meavaig. It was in spate. Water crashed over large rocks in loud white splashes. There was no crossing, though it was apparent from a brick pillar lying in the river that there had once been a bridge. (The 'Bridges' at Kinlochresort replaced "the ancient stepping stones" according to the Harris Mutual Improvement Association.) Just before entering Loch Resort the Abhainn Mhòr Cearn Resort was joined by an equally fierce river, the River Housar, which flows north from the south out of Glen Ulladale. Luachair, which included the game keeper's cottage, was to the west of the River Housar.

There was no question of crossing the river to the Harris side so a route south was ruled out. This was a pity as two wide glens fanned out southward, Glen Ulladale, dominated by the stunningly perpendicular Sròn Ulladale, and Glen Meavaig. Maps showed good tracks in both. A third, unnamed, glen went south east. This offered the only practical route to Bo'glas because it did not involve crossing any major rivers. Just beneath Creag Chterstir, at the top of the glen, I could join a track which would take me to Bo'glas and thence to Rhenigidale, my ultimate destination for the day. I sat with my back to the stone wall and drank my last coffee. It had taken me about three hours to get to Kinloch-resort from the estate gates, an hour and a half from the beehive houses.

The area I had just crossed is called 'Morsgail Forest' on the OS maps. The area to the south is marked as the 'Forest of North Harris'. The term 'forest' has a special meaning in England and I assumed that the same applied in Scotland. In medieval times a forest was an area where Forest Law applied. Such places were reserved for hunting by the King. Forests were not necessarily heavily wooded. In fact in England many are simply scrub and moor land, with copses to provide cover for the animals. This can be seen, for example, in the New Forest. Forest Law protected the game of the Forest. Stiff penalties including death once applied for breaches of Forest Law. I wondered if the same Forest Law applied in Scotland as in England. Were Scottish 'Forests' of the same antiquity as English 'Forests' or had English landowners of Scottish estates simply imported the term to give their estates a noble air? This might encourage their friends to think that the sport was good and deter the locals who might fear the worst.

After finishing my coffee I stood behind the house, out

of the wind and looked back across the moor I had just crossed. The Ordnance Survey 1:50,000 OS showed a track going in that directioin, north east from the back of the house. I decided to follow this track to see where it would lead. I crossed a field boundary, a grassed ridge through empty stone gate posts and came to the end of the track. I looked north across the moor. The compass bearing (40°) north to the hill to Scalaval Mula mirrored my route to the village. The moor ahead was flat and trackless but nearby was a low conical hill. From afar it looked like a chambered cairn but as I got closer the illusion faded. I climbed to the top of the hill. I was rewarded with a superb view across the unbroken moor, a landscape of tufts with rocky pinnacles. To the east the moor was bounded by the hills overlooking Loch Langavat in front of which Beinn a'Bhoth was prominent. I scanned the area. About a mile ahead on the horizon formed by conical hills, more or less on the 40° bearing, I thought I could see a post on a distant ridge. I checked with binoculars. Intrigued, I crossed the open moor to the post. There was no question of loosing line of sight as it was such a large post.

A skein of ten geese flew above me trying to head south but were blown east by the wind. Shortly after I saw them again, going north. I guess they had abandoned their southern flight for the time being. As I got closer to the ridge topped by the post I lost line of sight but found that I could, instead, align with a cairn on a prominent rock just beneath the post on the same 40° bearing.

When I got to the 'post' I was surprised to find that it was a large flat topped grey stone standing three to four foot above the moor. It was obviously a marker stone. It was an exciting find. The stone lined up directly with Glen Ulladale to the south and the nick on Scalaval Mula to the north. The cairn I had passed on the lower slope was indeed a sight marker to the stone. Here was clear evidence of navigation. At last I had found the old route to Kinlochresort.

The surrounding landscape was of small lochs amidst pointed hillocks. The lochs were part of the Lochan a Chilette Tuath chain. Two more standing stones were visible on rises to the north. Excited curiosity pulled me forward. I made for one beyond the peak on the next ridge. Before I got to it I came upon another stone angled upwards towards it. This summit stone had a point. Almost adjacent to it were two cairns set on rocks. Both looked like animals. The far one looked like a crouching frog, the near one like a smaller animal with eyes. Perhaps a mile on, I saw two other stones and then picked out two more stones on the same line.

About an hour and a half after leaving the village I got to a ridge from which I could see Morsgail Lodge. It looked mysterious in the distant mist on its lighter patch of green beside Loch Morsgail. The ridge was marked by a square stone from which the pointed stone to the south was clearly visible. As predicted from my map work, the line touched the end of the nearby loch. I tingled with excitement as I counted eight small stones set about fifty feet apart. They guided the route around the edge of the loch. Some of the dips in the peat also had stepping stones. One wonderful stone looked like a collar bone and had a band of coloured rock across it. Beyond the loch the route lead down into a small valley. At a sheltered spot it crossed the meander of a small burn by a stepping stone.

The large stones reappeared. One was ahead of a cairn of stones. Then there were two stones quite close together, one blotched with different colours of green, the other with a great white band through its top. I was guided across the top of the hill by more stones. Further on were two stones, the further of the two was just beneath a large mound with a greener top, surmounted by a tuft of grass blowing in the wind.

From here I picked up the track running north to the beehive huts. This took me down to the gnarled bridge by the huts. I had walked the line of the 1899/1964 route. Any doubts I had about the significance of the posts on the Lewis Moor disappeared. I was certain that they too were markers. Their locations appeared haphazard but I had little doubt, now, that they each had a purpose. They marked routes known only to those who had erected the markers. What a mystery to be solved!

I had crossed the wrong bridge this morning. If I had crossed the gnarled bridge and gone up the first grassy mound with the rounded top, the first of the chain of marker stones would have been visible.

Some months later I kicked myself as I sat in the august surroundings of the Modern Manuscripts Room at the Bodleian Library in Oxford. I was exploring the logs in Herbert Gatliff's papers. David Stone's 1965 log, *A Walker's Guide to Kinlochresort* gives a detailed description of the route from Morsgail to Kinlochresort including reference to the stones. He described it as "the postman's way to Kinresort". The bridge across the Abhainn a' Loin near Morsgail was still standing in 1965. After crossing the bridge, Stone recorded that

> The path continues due south for 2½ to 3 miles for much of the way and particularly beyond NB132200, it is extremely wet and uneven. Over the last 1½ miles the route is defined by standing stones, (mostly white painted) about a hundred yards apart, all in between being peat-hag; if the way is in doubt Loch

Beag Sheilabrie forms a useful landmark. When at length the stones peter out, in a kind of grass covered loch, Loch Resort is in full and magnificent view to the right and the quickest route to it is the straightest (provided dryness of foot is no object).

As I read Stone's log I re-lived the sense of fulfilment I had derived from my walk to and from Kinlochresort, and especially the discovery of the stones. I was sure that further evidence of navigation across these moors awaits discovery. This evidence of communication with the outside world was also the story of survival for such remote places. Walkers, like those who found their way to Kinlochresort, played their part in that story.

Stone obviously had a similar feeling at Kinlochresort:

One July evening I had walked over to Kinresort (sic), from Amhinnsuidhe via Glen Ulladale, and was invited in by the keeper on my arrival for a talk and a cup of tea; thus it was that I came to learn more of Kinresort's amazing story. How the heavy goods had to be brought by boat from Husinish, 10 miles round the coast and the lighter articles by post from Morsgail. How the postman had made the daily delivery for over fifteen years, summer and winter, and his predecessor, who had marked out the path across the moor, had held the job for three times as long, eventually being awarded the BEM. Then there were the telephone poles across that same moor and also at Tamanavay; they had been erected by the Army during the First World War, so that coastal observers could give immediate warning of German submarine intrusion; after the war an offer was made to sell the lines to the Post Office for £50 and was rejected. To-day only the poles remain as incongruous symbols of progress in a landscape that has remained unaltered in the last hundred years. I heard how the salmon fishing was the best in Harris, and the radio reception the best in the Western Isles; how the winters were rough, but snow rare; and about Kinresort's visitors: the keeper from Tamanavay once a week to collect his mail, the wealthy anglers from Stornoway and further afield, the Ordnance Survey men to paint the cairn on the top of Benisval and the occasional walker like myself, just passing through. Lonely life at Kinresort might be, but certainly never dull; that type of place breeds legends, and there are far more tales about it than I could hear in one evening or recount here.

Chapter 6

KINLOCHRESORT TO RHENIGIDALE

I PAID A second visit to Kinlochresort to confirm the route east to Bo'glas. The village and its milieu had made a big impression on me but on my second visit I found it more difficult to tear myself away. What are our modern cares and woes compared with the hardships endured by the people who used to live in this village? The example of their determination is etched on the walls of the village. Imagine their patience deployed out of expedience but so much part of the Hebridean character. The spirit of these people lives on instilled in this place. I was looking through a window in time. None of us would choose to return to these hardships but plenty wish to temper the stresses and strains of modern life by using the perspective of past experience.

Few expect to find wildernesses within the British Isles. Rather we think of Britain as a crowded land. But Kinlochresort is set in a vast wilderness. Why has the wilderness dropped out of the popular eye? Is it because it is out-with the norms of the market economy? Is it because wilderness is seen as unproductive waste land with no economic value, or no value that can be exploited for sufficient return?

The pleasures of the wilderness are solitary, inward almost, whilst the most popular pleasures of modern life are more sociable. They are accessible to all who have the mental and physical ability to visit, all who are willing and able to manage the risk and endure the privations.

For too long, especially in my youth, I had been put off exploring the wilderness by the toughies. These are the super fit characters who always seemed to appear in Youth Hostel common rooms. (They wash in cold water, eat nails and are scornful of all but their ilk.) For them the test had to be extreme to be worthwhile. One's own feats pale when compared to theirs (they were quick to tell you as much, if you gave them a chance). They always made the moor sound treacherous. Only they knew how to survive its rigours. These are secrets which, of course, they kept to themselves. Whilst their superior qualities rescued them from the bottomless bog you might not be so lucky.

The truth is that I had been deterred by lack of confidence, fear of the consequences of getting cold and wet. I was afraid of this unknown. Once I conquered this fear I found that the wilderness was manageable and rewarding. I had been deterred for too long. But not any more. Now the wilderness represented a frontier, a place where a new vision of life could be inspired. I realised that it was not such a bad place after all. The cold and wet could be kept at bay by adequate clothing and preparation. Interestingly I have not met the big talking 'toughie' type of my youth in the Hebrides. Perhaps I should not be surprised.

A visit to the wilderness certainly puts an interesting spin on the phrase applied to politicians who fall out of favour who are said to be 'in the wilderness.' Maybe they are banished but the wilderness offers them refreshment and the opportunity to re-order their thoughts.

About 100 years ago John Muir wrote about his trips in the wilderness areas of the USA to alert his adopted nation

to their value and the need to preserve their unique qualities. His writing inspired President Theodore Roosevelt to
establish the first National Parks. He recognised that wilderness is an important natural habitat as well as a breath-
ing space in modern society. The strengths of character
engendered by an understanding of the wilderness are important personal and societal attributes. It is pleasing that
the John Muir Trust, which keeps alive the flame of Muir's
thinking, is associated with the community purchase of the
North Harris Estate. The boundary of the North Harris
Estate is the southern boundary of the Morsgail Estate at
Kinlochresort.

My chosen route to the east was along the northern side
of the Abhainn Mhòr Cearn Resort river to the head of the
valley in Loch Chleistir. From there I could join a good
looking track to Bo'glas. The track had shown on pretty
well every OS map since 1882 and was on the contemporary 1:50000 map. This route did not cross any major rivers, though I would have to negotiate several tributaries, a
couple of which looked substantial. This was as well because
it was still impossible to cross the Abhainn Mhòr Cearn
Resort.

I took one last look at Kinlochresort. Cormorants were
drying their wings on a rock in the bay. The retreating tide
exposed banks of stone at the river outflow. A heron ambled
through the seaweed in the estuary; one or two gulls circled,
crying their whining call. The overhanging cliff at Glen Ulladale was crisp and the hill Sròn Ard in the next valley
east was equally prominent. The sun shone over the hills
of North Harris. Some rain came in over the hills ahead,
shrouding them in grey. I could still see blue sky to the west
but unfortunately, a rather cold rain began falling.

It was six miles from Kinlochresort to Bo'glas and the

A859. This was not too far but my progress would be slowed by nearly 500 metres of ascent in two separate climbs, after a descent to almost sea level. The river from the col at the top of the valley gushed loudly down the valley in places bumpy with glacial moraine. I passed the confluence of the Abhainn a'Chlair Bhig and Abhainn Mhór Cearn Resort rivers. (The latter came from the south.) Both were full and fast flowing which explained why the river was so fierce at Kinlochresort. The first tributary flowing from the north, the Alt Gil' a'Chlair Mhóir was the only difficult tributary I had to cross. After a short gorge, where I followed the river bank, the river turned south. I struck out across a flat area of moor to avoid the basket of eggs landscape of the moraine. A wren flew across my path and I saw a dipper ahead on the river bank. A fish jumped in the middle of the stream. Shortly afterwards, I saw a grouse. I thought I glimpsed Clisham. Ahead I had seen some rocks which looked like a cave. This turned out to be two huge erratics, with another jammed in between creating a shelter. I took a rest at the 'cave'.

From there I could see a large herd of deer grazing on the south side of the valley. A majestic stag stood on the brow of the valley side keeping look over his does. After setting off again I was surprised to come face to face with another stag, a large beast with fine antlers. It too took fright and ran off! As I continued upwards two golden eagles gave a superb flying display above the craggy cliffs which formed the eastern wall of the valley. They wheeled around and around above the crags on the side of Lurg a Mula.

By now the way was getting steep and the hummocky terrain was trying. I felt my age. But at least I was making progress. I was bucked by another exciting discovery on the opposite bank of the river, two intact beehive houses. They are marked on the 1973 edition but not on the 1997 edition of the Landranger map. I climbed down to them and with a little effort managed to jump the river which was, thankfully, not very wide. I realised that the houses were on a small island in the middle of the river. I crawled inside the bigger of the two. They were in superb condition. Inside this little house I was able to stand upright which meant that it was just over six feet high. The sun streamed through the cracks between the grey slabs of rock forming the cone. Maybe a small hole was left somewhere for the smoke from a fire. The top was off the bigger house; was this for the fire? It seemed to leave the interior too exposed considering the balance needed between providing an outlet for the smoke and preventing rain from entering. Maybe this one precious stone had been taken by the occupants when they abandoned the houses.

There were small well made cavities at the bottom of the wall. The entrance door was also well made and had a sound lintel. The house was surprisingly cosy. The other house was complete, but not quite so high. Maybe it was used as a byre, or store.

Back on the eastern bank I found a jumble of rocks marked with beautiful red lichen. They looked like ruins, maybe of burial chambers. Could they be shielings destroyed in the border dispute between Harris and Lewis in the hundred years before 1850? Whilst this dispute raged the rivals had destroyed each other's shielings. It was difficult to tell, but it demonstrated that the area had been subject to human influence for hundreds of years.

As the valley narrowed the river became more prominent. It clattered nosily over waterfalls created by rocky crags. One was a sheer band of rock about three feet high which ran across the whole river. At the head of the valley was a conical hill, obviously a pipe of moraine. The hill became my target. From its summit I got a wonderful view of the hills of Morsgail and Uig. The house at Kinlochresort on the Crola side of the river was visible on its carpet of green sward against the background of Benisval. From this perspective I could see a stream coming from the western side of Benisval.

To the north east of Benisval, I identified the hills Beinn a'Deas, Beinn Mhedhonach and Beinn a'Tuath above Morsgail Lodge. Directly west of Benisval lay the double line of the hills of Uig which I had identified from the Pentland Road: Teinnasval, Tahanaval, with Tarain in the foreground. Beyond these hills the most distant hill Mealisval which looked massive despite being nearly 11 miles away from my vantage point. Closer were Carcaval and Medieval Might. The Atlantic Ocean provided a sparkling back drop to this fine landscape.

I was disappointed to discover that the conical hill was not quite at the top of the valley. I had to continue upwards for another quarter of a mile before Loch Chleistir came in sight in the base of the col. I was relieved to see the line of the track going over the pass beyond the col. The sun was still shining but rain threatened. I heard a lowing noise but could see nothing. I assumed it was a deer.

I crossed the soggy ground of the col and climbed the final rise to the path. It had taken an hour and three quarters from Kinlochresort. Now on the track, I hoped that the worst part of the journey was over. My left foot was soaked and I was exhausted. I took a rest on a large rock by the track. Two stags looked down from the top of the ridge. I heard the lowing sound two or three more times. I had just crossed a text book corrie, a hollow beneath a ridge with a lake in it. Corries are created by glacial action. A small residual glacier at the top of a valley eventually wears a depression which becomes the lake. The glacial melt water helps to create a deep valley far deeper than the stream alone could have created.

I took the path to the top of the pass. At the top I left behind the hills of Uig and the superb view of the Atlantic Ocean. I faced the hills of Park for the first time. As I descended I tried to familiarise myself with the new landscape. I identified Beinn Mhòr and its associated hills in Park. Beinn Mhòr has a triangular shaped summit with flattened top and a lower summit to the south. Just to its north I assumed that the flat topped hill was Muaithabhal, north of which was Guainemol and Morr Mhonadh.

The pass took me between the towering crags of Stulaval to the south and Rapaire to the north rising to a height of about 330 metres. The track then descended to about 40 metres above sea level to cross the meandering Langadale River. It took me about half an hour to get down to the river. The path was sound, well made and about five feet wide. It crossed several loudly gushing streams. About half way down the last leg of the elongated zig zag there was a large boulder which I took to be a glacial erratic.

To the south the scenery was spectacular. At first Clisham was obscured by Mullach an Langa with the lower peak Tomnsival to the north. As I descended the southern end of the Langadale valley, at last, Clisham came into view. It was breath-taking. Closer, above me to the south, the skyline was dominated by steep rocky cliffs which rise to the summit of Stulaval. To the north, just beneath the pass I saw Cleit Earscliet with its almost flat summit on the northern shore of Loch Langavat.

I could see the path to Bo'glas as it climbed the eastern side of the valley. I was close to the river before I realised there was no bridge. The bridge stanchions were in place but the span was missing. Alongside the track to the north were the ruins of two or three stone buildings, perhaps more shielings destroyed during the border dispute. I chose my crossing point with care and some apprehension. The river was full, roaring in fact. A little downstream from where the bridge had stood was a small island. Stepping stones appeared to provide a way from the island to the far shore but the gap from the near shore to the island was just too wide. In the end I crossed just above the first bend beyond the 'bridge'. My stick was handy on the slippery rocks. On the other side, my dry towel proved the ultimate luxury. Afterwards my feet glowed from contact with the cold water.

The track ascended in zig zags like its counterpart on the western side. Near the summit I passed a cairn where another good quality track returned to the southern end of the Langadale valley. On the 1903 6 inch map this is shown extending to the upper part of the Langadale valley. Twenty five minutes after leaving the river I was at the top of the valley side. The hills of East Harris and the vast sea loch Loch Seaforth came into full view. Fiorabhal, in Park, looked splendid with one or two puffy clouds at its summit.

The track descended to Bo'glas along the northern side of the 'U' shaped Vigadale valley. I dropped quickly beneath the southern horizon formed by the valley side. Half way down I passed through the metal uprights of a gate and crossed a stream on stepping stones. It was easy walking and I got to the main road in about 30 minutes. I was now in Harris.

Harris

Harris is largely a rugged mountainous area joined to Lewis

along the boundary I had just walked. It is not an island. It is pinched in its middle by East and West Loch Tarbert, with the only town of Harris, Tarbert, in the middle. Its northern extent includes the beautiful North Harris hills with the Outer Hebrides' highest peak, Clisham. The southern part is equally rugged but with few of the spectacular hills common in North Harris. South Harris is better known thanks to the 'Golden Road', the dispute over the super quarry at Roineabhal and the *Castaway 2000* television series which was set on the island of Taransay off South Harris.

The track joined the A859 at right angles without ceremony, gate or fence. Although it is the only road linking Lewis with Harris it was a winding single track with no separate footway at this point. I dropped my pack and walked a short distance north along the road just beyond where a boundary sign proclaims "Harris" to get the awesome view along Loch Seaforth to the sea. The wide channel is flanked by steep slopes running straight into the sea. Northern Skye was visible beyond the mouth of the loch. Beyond Skye the mainland looked grey on the horizon.

Loch Seaforth is a fjord, a flooded U shaped glacial valley. It is six miles along the loch to the sea from Bo'glas. Rhenigidale is close to the mouth of the loch, a couple of headlands further south. It is another six miles north to the head of its furthest arm, at Seaforth Head. The Loch is about a mile wide for most of the distance to the sea but just east of Bo'glas it is about 1½ miles across because it accommodates a fair sized island, Seaforth Island. There are many tributary arms, one of which, Loch Maaruig, also widens Loch Seaforth considerably. I believe the loch was used for submarine training during the Second World War. It is large enough to accommodate a whole fleet of battleships.

I had thought that reaching Rhenigidale from Kinlochresort was ambitious. It had taken about 4 hours to cover six miles from Kinlochresort. It was at least as far again to Rhenigidale but the way was easier. I planned to walk along the A859 to the drove road, an old road which diverged on the slope of Caisteal Aird and then take the road to Rhenigidale.

I walked along the A859 through the small village of Bo'glas, making various stops to avoid passing traffic. (The road became a two lane highway in 2005.) The serene glory of Loch Seaforth provided the backcloth. About half a mile beyond Bo'glas I passed the Scaladale Activity Centre at the roadside. The modern building is a big improvement on the previous yellow painted corrugated building with its painted red window frames. This used to be run by the Northampton Association of Youth Clubs but in 1996 it was taken over by local youth organisations. They took the initiative and built this wonderful outdoor activity centre.

Beyond the Activity Centre the road widens to double width making my walk less hazardous. The power cables of the Harris/Lewis electricity connection strode past on their wooden poles. This project was one of the area's defining moments in the 1980s. An under-sea cable was installed from Skye to improve Stornoway and Lewis's power supply. I made steady progress along the road's elliptical curve over the Scaladale River and started up the slope of Caisteal Ard. The vista of the Scaladale valley before me revealed an arch of hills including Mullach an Langa, Mulla-fo-dheas, Clisham, Tomnaval, and Sgurr Scaladale. By now it was a sunny day.

As I walked up the A859 I could see the line of the drove road running straight along the western slope of Caisteal Ard. In 2001 it became the start of the Harris Walkway, a 26 mile walk via Tarbert to Meavig and Stockinish. It is 2 miles long and about ten feet wide, by far the widest track I had used since leaving the Butt of Lewis. The track was sound if a little rutted especially where holes had appeared in a few culverts but most were sound, their stone work still neat.

Once on the drove road tranquillity returned. The silent passage of occasional car, coach or lorry on the road below could not disturb or buffet me. To the north, Ardvourlie Castle looked picturesque amidst trees on the shores of Loch Seaforth. Built in 1863 as a sporting lodge it is now a smart hotel. The view across the Scaladale river gave uninterrupted views of Clisham. The rocky Sgurr Scaladale, cut by a stream down its face, stood in front of Clisham. To the north west, across the valley, the massive cliff of Creag Mò with scree (a sheet of loose rocks) was impressive. The sun shone on to the top of Mullach an Langa.

From the alignment of the drove road to the A859 it was clear that it had taken a different line up the hill from Ardvourlie to the modern road. John Murdo Morrison, the owner of the Harris Hotel, told me that the historic route crossed the Scaladale River closer to Ardvourlie than the modern bridge. The A859 is some four or five feet lower than the surface of the drove road.

The drove road turns south around a spur from the craggy Clett Ard. At 328 m it is dwarfed by Clisham at 799 m. At the top of the pass, (215 m), the craggy north side of Gormul Maaruig came into view on the west side of the valley. Toddun (528 m) also came into view ahead. It is the hill which dominates Rhenigidale. Dappled green in the sunshine, its side sparkled as sunshine glinted off the rocks. On and off since 1996 there has been a visitors' book on the summit of Toddun. Caitheshal (449 m), with a great gash down its side, ran almost sheer down on the northern side of Loch Seaforth. The northern tip of Skye was visible through the valley alongside Toddun.

I passed the telephone reflector just before getting to a loop of old road now by-passed by the modern road. The reflector is a large rectangular concave sheet of grey metal. A small transmitter huts stands alongside.

The drove road falls to about 170 m before joining the main road. The vista to the north is open giving splendid views of the hills of Park. There is a particularly fine view of Beinn Mhór (572 m). By this time of the day I was more interested in the view of the road to Rhenigidale. This too was visible passing along the valley at the foot of Toddun.

When I rejoined the A859 I was only a couple of hundred yards from the junction of the road to Maaruig and Rhenigidale. It had taken me 45 minutes from the start of the drove road and I estimated that two hours further walking would see me at Rhenigidale. I was tired but luckily there was only one arduous stretch ahead, the climb up to 170 metres into the last pass beneath Toddun.

The road to Maarvig left the main road and descended steeply for nearly a mile to a hairpin bend. The valley side it crossed was steeper and strewn with boulders. From the hairpin the old road to Tarbert continues along Glen Laxadale to Urgha as a green track before turning to Tarbert.

I made the turn to Maarvig and continued to the junction with the road to Rhenigidale. I was now on the shores of Loch Maarvig, a bay in Loch Seaforth. The Loch is home to several fish farms and provides anchorage for small boats. For some time one of the farms was used for experiments in night lighting to accelerate the growth of the fish. The lights cast an errie green/blue light in the pitch darkness. Today the boats in the bay looked pretty.

The asphalt road to Rhenigidale was completed in 1991.

It is a memorial to the determination of two men. The road was the dream of Roddy MacInnes, the owner and first warden of Rhenigidale Hostel. Roddy died in 1986 just after construction started. Kenny Mackay, Roddy's brother in law, then took up the cause. (Kenny was Councillor for Tarbert and North Harris from 1994 to 1999.) Both men knew that the road was the lifeline which would guarantee Rhenigidale's survival. Kenny was also instrumental in the fight for community ownership in North Harris.

Roddy was always willing to talk to hostellers about his dream. If this was over a dram of Crawfords Three Star whisky so much the better. He worked on the theory that humble hostellers had a habit of turning up later in life in more influential positions. One, John Hutchinson, who later became a road engineer, was responsible for carrying out the first survey of the route in 1977 under the auspices of the Schools Hebridean Society. Roddy gave hostellers an insight into a way of life where the basic necessities could not be taken for granted.

The Schools Hebridean Society ran summer expeditions for teenager school students for roughly thirty years. Each year the participants produced a report about their expedition. Rhenigidale was a favourite haunt. The Society pitched their marquee on the disused lazy beds beneath the Hostel and used the Hostel as a base. Dr Richard Young was chairman from 1986 to 1990 when the brave but sad decision was taken to wind up the Society because of declining interest. In the Society's final report he wrote,

> Overall the places we have visited have provided us with a taste, at least, of 'wilderness.' They have allowed us to discover things about ourselves and each other which are not easily possible at home. They have

enabled us to find out what are the really important things in our lives, both physically (a dry sleeping bag!) and within ourselves and each other.

Herbert Gatliff helped the Society in its early days. As a result when the Society was wound up in the late 1980s a residual £2000 was donated to the improvement of Rhenigidale Hostel. Rhenigidale got mains electricity in 1980. The wooden pylons were lifted in by helicopter. A picture of this operation, by Sam Maynard, records the operation in the book of poetry by Ian Stephen *Malin, Hebrides, Minches*.

By 1997 the single track asphalt road had got to the top of the pass between Toddun and Toscaram. To reach this point it had to negotiate the solid rocks of the hillside beneath the pass via hairpin bends of Alpine proportions. For some years there was no progress whilst negotiations over funding took place but in 1991 the road finally reached the village. From the pass it descends the final steep rocky slope into the village and sweeps round a final hairpin cut into the rock to reach the village.

I remember the area before the road. In 1978 my wife Petra and I walked out from Rhenigidale to Maaruig along the valley now used by the road. Whilst the valley floor was sound I could see that the last steep slope before Loch Seaforth was going to cause the road builders problems. It was largely rock with no easy way down. At the bottom of the slope we picked up a well constructed track threading its way to the two or three houses including one in ruins on the southern shore of Loch Maaruig before crossing the Maaruig River by a foot bridge. The last house before the Maaruig road is now at the first bend in the road. The house at Eilean-anbuich stands gaunt with its back to the road. It is well kept; maybe it is now a holiday cottage. A remnant of the track remains above the road but it now starts at the roadside opposite the house on the banks of the Maaruig River as the bridge over the river is down.

As I trudged round the sweeping bends designed to ease the climb for motor vehicles, I knew what Richard Young meant. The idea of that cuppa and a shower at Rhenigidale seemed awfully good. In the valley in the shadow of Toddun the road passes three lochs in a straight stretch. Lochan an Fheór is followed by Loch Mór and then Loch Beag. Todden towered above the road.

As I emerged from the side of Toddun the fish farm in Loch Trollamarig came into view. This used to be accompanied by a grim grey painted old coaster but it sank in a storm in 1996. I thought this poetic justice because the boat disturbed the whole balance of the scene. The fish farm was intrusive but it blended more readily into the scenery that the coaster. The coaster had been used for automatic feeding but I heard that the fish were just too clever. They discovered how to open the feeding traps, despite the machine! The company now sends in a feeding team by boat from Maaruig twice a day by boat. The old coaster has been left to rot on the seabed where it sank.

I crossed the cattle grid with care and flew down the last slope into Rhenigidale. After the last hairpin I could see the Hostel across the valley. The door was open. Smoke rose from the chimney.

Getting to the village is always a thrill. No more so than today. That cup of tea was ambrosia.

Chapter 7

HARRIS – THROUGH THE WINDOW IN TIME

WAKING AT RHENIGIDALE always fills me with confidence and joy. I drank my morning coffee sitting on the seat at the front of the Hostel looking over the sea to Skye. Distant ships passed silently in the Minch. My route had taken me 96 miles from the Butt. I believed it would be a little over 30 miles to Leverburgh, a distance I aimed to walk in two days.

The Gatliff Hostel has been in the village since 1962 and played an important part in its survival. It acts as an embassy from which the outside world can establish a relationship with the community in Rhenigidale. Rhenigidale has always seemed like the edge of the world. The backdrop of Skye and the distant mainland increases that sense of remoteness. The companionship with other hostellers at Rhenigidale is real. Until 1989 hostellers slept in camp beds under the eves of the tin roof and gained access to the sleeping platform by ladder. On my first visit in 1973 water was drawn from a well and the toilet was a chemical elsan which had to be emptied daily into the sea. The well is still there, though unused. Today there is a flush toilet, a shower and hot running water. In 1973 there was no electricity so hostellers had to know how to light oil or Tilley lamps or, if not, use candles until Roddy MacInnes, the warden, came along to light a lamp.

In 1992, after refurbishment, the Hostel was re-opened by Magnus Magnasson KBE, then Chairman of Scottish Natural Heritage. It is now looked after by Alasdair Mackay and his wife Kathy, who live next door.

Rhenigidale was the first Hostel established by Herbert Gatliff's newly formed Gatliff Trust. Herbert recorded that in its infancy the Trust was "a quite small trust, to pay a few pounds a year to the two churches where his father had been vicar and a few bodies with which he had been specially associated." These included the National Trust and the National Trust for Scotland. He said, "It was to have an income of £30 a year, rising perhaps to £50, which would provide a little margin for emergencies."

Soon after starting the Trust Herbert agreed to support a simple Youth Hostel at Rhenigidale. During the summer of 1961 Mac Hoskin, a volunteer warden at Achininver Hostel and an active member of Epsom and Ewell YHA Local Group, visited Rhenigidale at Herbert's suggestion. Herbert had heard that there were some empty houses in the village. One, owned by Roddy MacInnes, a local crofter, proved suitable for use as a hostel. Roddy was enthusiastic about the project and the Hostel opened at Easter in 1962.

The SYHA did not 'recognise' the Hostel until 1987. Instead they handed over the fund created to establish a hostel in the Hebrides as a memorial to Keith Chambers, a London caver and Chairman of London Region YHA, who had visited the Outer Hebrides in 1951. Keith drowned on a coastal climbing weekend in Cornwall in 1955. The fund provided an income of £25 per year. I have heard a different version of this story, that Herbert Gatliff had given the SYHA £500 specifically to establish a hostel in the islands.

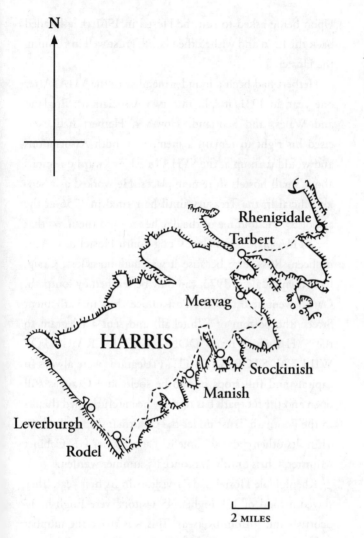

Figure 7 Rhenigidale to Leverburgh, South Harris

Upon being asked to run the Hostel in 1961 they handed back the fund and wished the Gatliff Trust well in running the Hostel.

Herbert had been a founder member of the YHA. After one year, in 1931, it split into two Associations: England and Wales, and Scotland. However, Herbert had exercised his right to remain a member of both Associations and would turn up at the SYHA to ask awkward questions about small hostels in remote places. He worked as a senior official in the Treasury until he retired in 1956 at the age of 55. He told me of the day he received the news that the SYHA planned to close Craig Youth Hostel near Achnasheen, Ross-shire because it was making a loss. Craig, like Rhenigidale in 1973, can only be reached by footpath. Gatliff went across to the Post Office then in Parliament Street (the bottom of Whitehall) and sent a telegram to the SYHA which read, "DON'T CLOSE CRAIG STOP WILL PAY STOP GATLIFF". (Telegrams were always in capitals and full stops had to be spelt out.) Craig is still open and the footpath has recently been refurbished thanks to the Footpath Trust under the Chairmanship of Andrew Thin. Its other claim to fame is that a former UK Cabinet Minister, Chris Smith, was once its summer warden.

Rhenigidale Hostel had 71 visitors in its first year. They stayed a total of 161 nights. 45 visitors were English, 17 Scottish and 9 from overseas. This was twice the number Herbert Gatliff had thought likely. The YHA provided the equipment for the Hostel and publicised the Hostel. The Hostel had a log book, like all hostels, but unlike other hostels this was "not of a standard pattern" since it had space for remarks. Hostellers soon took up the silent invitation to append remarks and soliloquy. "I've been to over 100 hostels and this is the best that I have ever stayed in", wrote one. This log book, together with Hostel log books from the other Gatliff Hostels, is now in the Local History Library in Stornoway.

Before the road, getting to Rhenigidale always meant walking to the village and being prepared to stay for a few days. People stayed until their food ran out. At times people staggered into Rhenigidale carrying massive packs. The lucky ones met someone in Tarbert who was going to the village by boat. Over the years I had spent a lot of time exploring the area, sometimes visiting places like the deserted village of Molinginish, on other occasions just sitting quietly taking in the haunting silent beauty of Loch Seaforth with its shores rising steeply out of the water. In 2000 the Gatliff Hebridean Hostels Trust published a guide to Rhenigidale area by Neil Pinkett. In 2002 the Gatliff Trust held a walk from Tarbert to commemorate the fortieth anniversary of the Hostel.

In 1974 *Country Life* carried a feature on Harris, which described the walk from Tarbert to Rhenigidale as "perhaps the finest path in Britain." The path is justifiably popular in the islands and is described in a Western Isles Tourist Board leaflet. It is a recognised detour on the Harris Walkway. However, for the moment, it is little known in the rest of Britain. There are wonderful views of the Shaint Islands from the path. These are the islands described by Adam Nicolson in his book *Sea Room*.

Rhenigidale is said to have been settled by people who originally came from the more fertile west side of Harris. This mirrors the history of the Bays of Harris. In 1903 Rhenigidale had a population of 89. At that time there were seven crofts in Rhenigidale with two or three houses on each.

The rugged terrain of the area made land communication difficult but villages clustered around coastal bays could receive goods by sea and fish the inland waters. Puffers brought coal while communication with Tarbert was maintained by the men's open fishing boats.

As on every other visit to Rhenigidale I wished that I could have stayed longer but I was keen to be on my way south. I retraced my steps half a mile up the road and joined the path to Urgha from where I would walk into Tarbert. Its junction with the road is marked by a local authority sign "Tarbert" (and a hand painted sign to the Hostel the other way) just before a metal crash barrier. The path dropped away from the road quickly. Fairly soon after leaving the road I passed a set of ruins on the slope between the path and the sea. This was Gary-altoteger, a deserted village. The outline of the village lazy beds was visible. Neil Pinkett comments that the buildings closest to the shore were built as a shop and storeroom for the area as they could be supplied by sea.

After Gary-altoteger the path goes through a wicket gate and crosses a bridge over a burn. It regains height and crosses another burn in a deep cleft by a wooden bridge. Trees and bushes grow in the gully. The path then makes a long descent before climbing over an area of flat rock. Here the track disappears but the route is marked by stone cairns. Beyond the flat rock the path resumed and went past a huge glacial erratic boulder on the side of the track. It then turns sharp left before making the final descent to Loch Trollamarig. All along the path the views to the mainland and northern Skye are superb.

Loch Trollamarig is a bay enclosed in high walls. A burn from a step rocky valley runs across a rocky beach. I went to the shore for a breather before tackling the zig-zags. From the beach a feint track is visible. This goes to Molinginish, a deserted village on the southern shore of Loch Trollamarig. I resisted the temptation to take that route. It was a detour, passable with a scramble including jumping two burns, one with a small waterfall. Instead I took the zig zags up the steep wall of the bay.

From sea level the path climbs almost vertically 600 feet by twelve hairpin turns, hence its familiar name, the 'zig zags'. The first leg is long and tiring. The second leg is demoralising because it is even longer. I took a rest at the end of the second leg as no heroics were necessary. However, I did not take off my pack as the manoeuvre needed to put it back is too risky on this slope.

The next three legs are short but the sixth leg is a long steep pull. As I made the turn I thought "half way". I had never been able to walk the zig zags without counting and today was no exception. The following four legs are short but this is little consolation, as each is steep. The drop over the edge of the path at this point is nearly vertical. The final leg was long after which there is a further 200 or 300 feet to the summit. The erosion of the path is particularly bad at the top of the zig zags but at least it is possible to walk in the heather alongside. Just before the summit the path from Molinginish joins from the east.

From the summit there is a fine view to the south over East Loch Tarbert and the Bays of Harris. The mainland to the north of Ullapool is also visible. The path descends down the rock strewn slope of Beinn Tharsuinn into the valley of the Abhainn an t-sratha. As the path takes a straighter course it has to cross the burn twice. I felt as if I was descending a series of shelves, each over a rocky ledge. The track joins the road at Urgha. From here it was an easy walk into Tarbert along the Tarbert to Scalpay road.

It had taken me four hours to get to Tarbert. Tarbert

stands at the confluence of East Loch Tarbert and West Loch Tarbert. The two lochs are separated by an isthmus only half a mile wide and on the map it looks as if South Harris hangs beneath the broader North Harris on a thread. Tarbert has always been a ferry port and natural focal point for Harris. Today boats cross to Tarbert from Uig in Skye

Tarbert is neat but it always reminds me of the Klondike as its houses and shops, interspersed by a few trees, jostle with rocky outcrops. The modern Tourist Information Centre welcomes visitors on the pier. Just opposite is a general hardware stores where it is still possible to buy all manner of hardware long forgotten down south such as paraffin fuelled Tilley lamps and hand held shears for sheep shearing.

I lingered for a pleasant lunch in the Harris Hotel. This Hotel is a testimony to John Murdo Morrison. He recently passed control to his daughter, Sarah. John Murdo Morrison is a renowned Gaelic singer. He has laboured long and hard to help Harris. He was the tower of strength behind the Harris Mutual Improvement Association and is now associated with the Harris Development Company. Harris Development spawned the Harris Walkway Initiative.

From Tarbert I aimed to walk through the Bays of Harris. The Bays of South Harris are on the east side of the island. They came into existence after Harris was sold to Alexander Macleod of Berneray in 1779. He cleared the machair areas of west Harris for sheep farms and relocated the population to the villages of the Bays. There he built harbours and piers and settled fishermen from the West Coast of Scotland. After the kelp industry collapsed the area was considered over populated. Kelp is seaweed collected and burned to create a mineral rich powder for use as fertiliser.

I climbed out of Tarbert along the A859 road to Leverburgh. This is the beginning of the road from Tarbert to

Rodel built in 1920. It goes up the western side of East Loch Tarbert opposite the pier where the ferry MV Hebrides was now anchored. The old path starts at a bolted wooden gate. It climbs more steeply than the road and quickly sheds its influence. This is the gateway to a labyrinth of paths running through South Harris. The area is rich in paths with much of the old network intact. So rich that I could have spent several days exploring and mapping the paths but my goal was simply to find a route to Leverburgh. By walking the time honoured way I was to see South Harris as I had never before seen it.

Since my first days in Harris in the 1970s I had suspected that a labyrinth of tracks had existed in the islands. Today I discovered that this was correct, but that many had been lost. Some had been overlain by tarmaced roads. The Rhenigidale path was, indeed, typical of paths to be found. They were well made because they were the only means of communication between townships or remote crofts. Many radiated from schools, like the path I had found at Tolsta Chaolais in Lewis.

The track leaving Tarbert was three to five feet wide on a stone and pebble base. Like the drove road it is part of the Harris Walkway. The path was followed, loosely, by the overhead electricity power lines and buried services. In fact it was the presence of the concrete marker posts which indicated the existence of buried services that often gave the clue to the existence of a path. The posts carried a variety of metal letters: "AV", "ScV" or "W" were common.

In the 1920s the County Council 'adopted', that is took responsibility for, the road from Tarbert to Rodel and started improving it, a process which has continued until the present day. Some stretches of path such as the one I was currently walking along had been by-passed by the road.

At one point the road suddenly reappeared about 100 feet below the path, as its more level route had been created by blasting. A blue four wheeled drive pickup truck went along the road. A pair of mallards flew across Loch Direcleit some way beneath the road.

The path then passed a string of houses and continued until the track and road merged. The track offered picturesque insights into old Harris. Near a small deciduous tree, an unusual sight in Harris, I saw a small red roofed building, plainly a former thatched cottage, with a tap at the front door. A heavy piece of flat metal from a stove held the door shut. The roof of the byre beside the former thatched house was partly collapsed revealing a jumble of fish boxes inside.

Thankfully there was little traffic despite it being the only road between Tarbert, Rodel and Leverburgh. I walked along the single track road. Ahead was a bleak rocky landscape decorated with a plethora of poles and cables bearing translucent green insulators. Here the old road had been subject to improvement. I followed a loop of old road now cut off by a straighter new road, which gave me some relief from the threat of traffic, but I was brought back to the current road all too soon. Usefully it took me to just where, according to the map, the old track to Meavag leaves the road. Right on cue a Harris Walkway sign appeared. I walked down the stone chipped tarmaced drive to a house (Cearnn Dibig) by the shore I could see the path continuing along the foreshore beyond the house.

I could only guess at the age of the path. It took a fairly straight course along the foreshore crossing headlands and passing ruined houses. Now rising then falling, going through empty gate posts passing through fences, past old lazy beds, past all the artefacts of a modern crofting life grafted on to the old ways. One of the ruined houses had been turned into a sheep fank. The sea was ever present, ever noisy, blue green and clear as it lapped the rocks close to the shore frothing up on little sandy patches between the rocks. Wild life was abundant including diving ducks and seals curious about my passing. I saw the occasional heron in lugubrious flight across the sea from fishing point to fishing point.

The geology of the area was vividly displayed alongside the path. On the stretch before Meavag I passed along the front of an overhanging cliff. Strips of pink granite intruded in the grey rock with heather growing in the crevasses. Beneath the path, right by the shore, was another overhang cut by the same pink granite. On the foreshore white rocks were marked red and black by the sea. Shortly after I passed a great chunk of stone with patches of white and green lichen. I walked over a slab bridge with the water falling over a stone and a clump of miniature fern in the hollow. Offshore were small islands no more than rocky outcrops, black beads in the water. A fish farm appeared in the bay.

The quality of the path varied. Some patches were covered with asphalt. Later it reverted to a pebble based path. In other places the path was eroded and crumbling. I passed two grey-rendered houses sheltered at the head of an inlet and obscured from general view by large evergreen trees. A six wheeled Agro-cat sat in an outhouse with a red keeled rowing boat on a trailer. The garden was well tended with bushes overhanging the stream.

Meavag came into view. Smoke was rising from the chimney of the first house. I knew I had entered the village when the path went through an empty gate post – the village gate – and then meandered from house to house. This brought a series of encounters with back doors many still with adjacent standpipes, both out of keeping with the habits of modern life.

Meavag was quiet, like all the townships in South Harris today but a few inhabitants were going about their business. There are one or two modern bungalows, a renovated traditional house but other houses stood in ruins. Older buildings, perhaps former thatched houses, served as byres or garages for tractors or cars. Elsewhere piles of stones were all that remained of thatched houses. Intact byres seemed to contain a jumble of old nets and fish boxes, bits of rusting iron, maybe flakes of crumbling corrugated iron, gnarled wood, former roof trusses. Just as in Ness I saw houses abandoned full of decaying furniture.

Thanks to the Walkway project the bridge over a deep burn has been replaced allowing direct access from the path to Meavag Pier. At the Pier men in fork lift trucks were loading paletted tanks and feeds into supply boats for the off-shore fish farms.

I continued along the single track 'Golden Road' the mile or so to Drinishader. After climbing the hill beyond Meavag I was out on to the rocky open moor. There was no traffic. A young couple pushing a child in a push chair came towards me, a welcome symbol of hope. We exchange cheery "hellos". I wondered if the youngster, when grown up, would show the same commitment to the area as its parents or whether, like so many today, would see the future elsewhere.

The 'Golden Road' refers to the road which winds its way through Meavag, Drinishader, Plocrapool, Scadabhagh, Grosebay and Stockinish. Work began in April 1947 and was completed in January 1951. It joins the Tarbert to Rodel road at the Stockinish road end.

I wondered why the Meavag to Stockinish road is called

'Golden'. It is certainly not paved with gold and, being on the east coast of the island, it cannot refer to the legendary Hebridean sunsets. I wondered if it referred to the beauty of the views or was it an allusion to the wealth it was hoped that the road would bring to the area? The appellation certainly encourages tourists to take the circular coach trip (actually the timetabled service) from Tarbert down the west side returning via Rodel and the 'Golden Road' to Tarbert. James Shaw Grant gives one explanation. He says the name was ironic, "given by the locals to mark the anguish of a remote and grudging authority over the cost of providing the road".

The truth appears to be less romantic. Bill Lawson, Harris's respected resident historian and genealogist, maintains that the term was one of abuse levelled by a London daily newspaper at the cost of constructing the road over such difficult terrain. Thankfully southern views appear to have changed, as witnessed by the fact that the Scalpay bridge was opened by Tony Blair in 1997, the first serving Prime Minister to visit the islands. I had good views of the bridge all the way from Tarbert to Drinishader.

The island of Scalpay is some four miles to the east across East Loch Tarbert. As I walked through Drinishader I could see a large boat aground on the southern rocks of the island. The pitch of the waves was causing its rusty white/cream superstructure to bob up and down. Later I learned that the ship, loaded with road stone, had gone aground in 1996 in good weather. Apparently the Scalpay fishermen offered to tow it off the rocks but the owners declined awaiting approval from their insurance company. In the mean time a gale blew up and the boat was lost.

I walked off the moor into Drinishader township. The houses surround a picture postcard bay. A red hulled fishing boat was at anchor. It also has a typical Hebridean village Post Office and General Stores in grey corrugated iron with a red roof. At the head of the bay sat a pile of wooden slatted fish boxes, resting on a yellow fish box marked "Newlyn". Other fishing gear, buoys and creels, lay around at the edge of the road.

I continued along the road towards Plocrapool past Drimshader school with its corrugated iron outhouses. The road passed a caravan with a dinky garden replete with pots plants, model birds and animals. A plastic plover sat on top of a mast. Caravans or 'mobile homes' as they are more honestly known, are common in many rural areas including the islands but are often hidden away. Many are in permanent occupation, a sign of rural homelessness. Shortly afterwards I passed some lazy beds, one still in cultivation.

My aim was to take the old footpath to Grosebay. It left the road at the top of Loch Plocrapool. I was sorry not to be passing through Plocrapool because it is an important local spot, the home of the late, Marion Campbell. She was a legend in her lifetime because she wove Harris Tweed on a double width wooden loom. She did much to keep the industry alive and was a popular tourist stop on the 'Golden Road'. Her son has carried on the tradition.

Harris Tweed is a hand woven cloth of unrivalled warmth, natural beauty and durability. The famous Orb Mark on the Harris Tweed label is a registered Trade Mark. In 1993 a Harris Tweed Authority was set up by Act of Parliament to protect and promote the material. The wool is produced, spun, dyed and finished in the Outer Hebrides. Tweed weaving was a traditional activity of hearth and home in the islands. It was developed as a commercial activity in the mid-nineteenth century thanks to the inspiration of the Dowager Countess of Dunmore, Catherine

Herbert. A daughter of the Earl of Pembroke, the Countess of Dunmore was a member of the family which then owned Harris. (Leverhulme also tried to develop the industry in the 1920s.)

The fortune of the Harris Tweed industry is subject to vagaries of fashion and economic cycles. I have two Harris Tweed jackets which I wear with pleasure but I am often the only person wearing the material even at island gatherings. One exception was at an event attended by the islands' Member of the Scottish Parliament, Alasdair Morrison. He was wearing the plaid together with a jacket and waistcoat in fetching green Harris Tweed. I am sad that the material is not more popular. I believe it is superior material for keeping out the elements and lasts longer than the synthetic alternatives but it is too heavy for many sports. Sadly, tweed has a rather staid image which is regarded as 'out of fashion.' In the south it is often too warm to wear tweed for every day activities, especially with centrally heated buildings.

The path to Grosebay ran across the hummocky rocky terrain north of Loch Plocrapool. It was about three feet wide and easy to follow. A white hulled rowing boat lay by the loch ready for the gillie. Ahead a crofter with his dog tended his sheep. The path crossed a burn by a wooden bridge with wooden hand rails and went through a gate. It then crossed a rocky area where it became braided, its route marked by stone cairns. At the top of the hill I believe I glimpsed the conical peak of Taransay twelve miles to the north west. The island is now famous as the setting for the TV programme *Castaway 2000*.

The path reached a junction. I could see from the map that one way went to Scadavay, the other to Grosebay. I turned towards Grosebay and continued through a gate at a raised stone boundary marker. The gate was made of four slates and was closed by chain linked to a nail. The short track took me to the road to Grosebay. Just before the road it crossed a dinky concrete footpath bridge. I had to displace a sheep standing imperiously astride the bridge.

The mile into Grosebay went through a typical undulating grey rocky Harris landscape dotted with sheep, heather and lochs. Some lochs had small islands covered with dwarf trees or scrubby bushes. Other lochs had patches of white water lilies. Electricity lines picked their way between the lochs. The sea loch, Loch Grosebay, on the left side of the road, intruded right into the heart of the village. I came to the road junction where two mobile homes stood surmounted by brown freezes. Opposite was a field of chickens.

"Loch Grosebay" is also the name given to a fresh-water loch which lies to the west of the road in the heart of the village. According to my map-work the path to Stockinish went south west from the southern tip of the freshwater loch. I could see the old path as it threaded its way house to house opposite the loch before crossing another of the small cast concrete footbridges across the burn flowing from Loch Grosebay. It continued up the rocky slope on the opposite side of the road.

Soon I was walking towards Stockinish past iris beds. The path was obvious. It went through empty gate posts in fences past the ruin of a house and the junction with another path to an occupied house. The path undulated through two miles of rocky crags.

The route of the path gave fine views of the hills of North East Harris. Looking back, Grosebay stood out on a carpet of green against the brown moor. After the path passed through a gully it made its way round the end of Loch Mhic Neacail and crossed two burns. The bridge over the first has recently been replaced by the Harris Walkway. Beyond was higher ground with low rocky cliffs. The 1882 map showed a path crossing from the north on its way to Cluer. That way looked passable being largely grassy, though the course of the path had become overgrown.

I climbed into this higher, rocky area and found that it contained an interesting jumble of green, pink, yellow and brown rocks. At the summit I got my first glimpse of the southern Harris skyline dominated by Roineabhal (460 m). The path went down a steep slope to a braided stream with two flat stone bridges side by side. The stream continued down towards Cluer through a deep gorge with scraped rock on one side and crags on the other. The lie of the land meant that progress along the path provided a changing panorama as distant houses popped into view and then disappeared. I guessed some were on the 'Golden Road' passing through Cluer. I went through a series of gates in fences and dry stone walls, passed the back door of a croft house and arrived at the former Hostel. This was not surprising as the building was a school before it opened as a Youth Hostel in 1963. It closed in 1998 having been unable to survive in the face of a plethora of bunk houses that had developed in south Harris. (Some have since disappeared.)

As my day in South Harris progressed I came to appreciate the dignity with which contemporary Harris lived with the hardships of its history and geography. This increased my admiration for Bill Lawson, Kenny Mackay, John Murdo Morrison and their ilk. This understanding was paralleled by the optimism I felt in my youth. In later life this had been moderated by the realisation that injustice is common and that hardship almost always follows injustice. In the 1840s Harris had been devastated by potato blight. Many had left the area for the New World. Others lived on what food they could glean from the foreshore. Although a history of injustice and hardship may be close to the surface the fact that the people of South Harris just get on with their lives without complaining is the real lesson to guide one in modern life.

Stockinish to Leverburgh

It was 16¼ miles from Tarbert to Stockinish, enough for one day's walk. From Stockinish to Rodel I anticipated more difficulty in finding a route. According to the map there appeared to be less tracks. I guessed that many had been obliterated since 1920 by improvements to the Tarbert to Rodel road. The way south was more straight-forward because the coastline to Rodel was less indented than the coastline from Stockinish to Tarbert. South of Stockinish the bays landscape gave way to a more level moor pockmarked with lochs and lochans. South of Manish a basin shaped moor was dominated by Roineabhal to the south and Coileach to the West.

To resume my progress south I walked east from the old school to the Stockinish road end. Initially the terrain to the east of the road was rocky but once the landscape softened the old path became evident as it ran from the old school through modern fields divided by fences. Eventually the track and road crossed but it was still possible to see the path running to the west of the road. Beyond, to the west of the road, is the sea loch, Loch Stockinish.

From the junction of the Stockinish and Rodel roads the track continued straight across the moors for half a mile. The first part was a tarmaced township road to a sheep fank after which it narrowed and passed through two gates. It continued to a junction with a path which ran parallel to the road. Ahead was a loch and on its shores an upturned green hulled boat. All around were expanses of wonderful wild, empty, open moor with purple heather. I turned south. The path was well constructed and crossed the occasional burn by the standard small concrete bridges with their solid balustrades. Unfortunately in places the path was badly eroded and covered in heather. Jutting rocks diverted its route. In other places the rocks created a large step which had to be negotiated. These rocks made the path impossible for cyclists. A hooded crow watched me, matching my progress along the path by flying from rock to rock.

Ahead were the hills Maoladh Mhicearraig and Ceann Reamhar na Sroine. The later, to the west, had a cairn on its summit. These hills are part of the chain which creates a south east to north west axis across the island.

The track took a straight course to the head of Stockinish Bay. To get to the house at the bay head the track went down a steep slope of some fifty feet using a hair pin bend. A Tourist Board way-marked track strode north-west along the glen to Seilebost on the beautiful west coast. This is said to be a 'coffin route', a route along which people from the east returned their dead for burial in their traditional cemeteries on the west coast.

The house at the head of the bay stood on a loop of track now isolated because the road goes over the bay closer to the sea on a green painted metal bridge. A picturesque cliff forms the northern wall of the bay. I walked along the loop stranded by the road.

I continued south along the road but the old path appeared on alternate sides of the road like bits of rope. The concrete utility markers provided clues to its existence. Only where the sections of the path were large or at a distance from the road, for example just south of Bayhead, at Manish, at Ardvey and at Lingerbay, was it worth using them. I soon encountered the first such section, just south of the head of Stockinish bay, where the old track veered off up a steep hill as the road climbed alongside Loch Sàile. The slope was marked with small stone cairns.

The road was single track with a wide verge on either side. There was virtually no traffic. At one point it passed through a short valley enclosed with cliffs. A massive spider's web replete with a spider with awesome black and brown stripped legs hung from the cliff face. The road pressed against the cliff to skirt a small loch which occupied most of the valley. At the top the cliff diverged from the road and continued towards the sea where a pretty fresh water loch stood at its foot. In the bay to the south was a massive fish farm. There was a good view of the islands south of Quidnish across the bay. In a passing place on this road, a small house had been built; was it a toy or was it a home for the little people? (I thought they only lived in Ireland.) Then I passed some lazy beds one of which was obviously sown with potatoes. The track to Ardslave was still visible running off to the east.

I walked to Manish school, closed in 2000. My map-work showed that there was a worthwhile loop of old track going around an enclosed sea loch south of Manish school but I had difficulty finding its start. Standing in front of the southern wall of the school I picked up a clue, two concrete utility posts. They crossed a dank open area of ground. A burn ran from this dank area though a narrow valley. I followed the markers. To my surprise I came across a slab bridge and then a track running down the narrow valley. I found a line of stones and the remains of a bridge. From this point the track became more evident going over a series of rocks positioned like a staircase down the steep slope. The valley opened at the side of the loch and I found myself in the midst of a deserted village overgrown with ferns and trees. All was still. The village was completely isolated from the road. A wren flew across my path. I tingled with excitement.

The path went from house to house in the old way. It took me around the loch to a point where a line of stones indicated a route. A heron flew low over the loch. Lines of stones guided me across a rather boggy area then through an area of ferns until eventually I picked up a feint track. This grew bolder, crossed two well made stone embankments, until it rejoined the road. Below one was the decaying hull of a large wooden boat jammed into a cleft of the rock. Its engine lay exposed in the open hull. At high tide I guessed the hull would be semi submerged.

Roineabhal began to assert itself on the horizon, proud like a white knight. It appeared to have two summits divided by a wedge shaped cleft slashed by a white line. As I got closer I could see that the line was light glinted off a gushing stream.

Roineabhal is predominantly anorthosite, a hard white rock streaked with black set with green, red and brown/red fragments. Are the red fragments garnets? For years controversy reigned over Roineabhal after a large aggregates company wanted to excavate about a quarter of the mountain for use as road stone. Eventually, planning permission was refused. The resulting quarry would have created a tidal basin big enough to load stone into sea going ships. The quarry would have created employment in the area but environmental concerns overrode this argument. However it would have been sure to hit other businesses, especially places like the enterprising new Rodel Hotel and the smart Scarista House Hotel on the beautiful west side of the island.

To reach Roineabhal I had to cross a wide boggy basin about five miles east to west and three miles north to south. The road south meanders across the area to avoid rocks. The basin is created between the hills An Coilleach, Heilavsa-bhal Mor in the north, Bulabhall, Bleaval and Mùla to the west and Roineabhal to the south. Just beneath Mùla is the largest loch in the area, Loch Langavat 2½ miles long and ½ mile wide at its widest point. (The Loch of same name in Lewis, just north of the border of the Harris border, is nearly eight miles long.).

Ardvey stands about a mile north of Roineabhal. To reach Ardvey the road crosses a deep but narrow inlet by a bridge. Before the bridge was constructed it was safer to by-pass the inlet rather than cross the burn flowing over the slabs of rock. In winter, when the river was in spate it was particularly dangerous, according to James Shaw Grant.

To make the detour (of about a mile) to avoid the inlet, the track crosses the boggy moor and picks its way between the lochs. It crosses several streams by wooden plank bridges and goes through a number of gates. To regain the road west of Ardvey I had to turn sharp south and climb stone steps beside a house. This put me on the road to Leverburgh which skirts to the north of Roineabhal. I returned the 150 yards or so to the Ardvey junction to continue south to Rodel.

South of Ardvey, in Finsbay, I passed a sign offering sce-nic trips round the bay and just beyond a boat builder in a shed with a semi circular tin roof. A couple of boats were on blocks outside.

Right on cue a track looped off to the east round Loch na Criadhach. Thinly scattered reeds grew in the loch. An up-ended white hulled boat lay on its shore. The pebble based track was about 4 feet wide and crossed a small burn using a low stone embankment. It reached a gate at Ceann a Bhaigh under a cliff face. Much tumbled rock was scat-tered at the foot of the cliff. I walked through Lingerbay township and rejoined the road to Rodel. One house had a miniature house in its garden flanked by a gnome, mole and a miniature phone box.

I emerged in the shadow of Roineabhal. The road to Rodel twisted through foothills and passed several small quarries and some scruffy derelict concrete buildings. The road side was littered with chunks of anorthosite. I breasted the top of a hill. Directly ahead was the wide expanse of the southern Minch between Skye and Uist. The craggy outcrops of Renish Point, the most southerly point of Harris, and the distant shore of North Uist came into view. From here the road to Rodel was straight and double width but still devoid of traffic. It passed buildings once used as a Coast Guard lookout point. Silence was broken only by the wind singing in cables on wooden poles marching down the hill parallel to the road.

Rodel is a spot of considerable antiquity. It is an ancient harbour in an enclosed inlet just north of Loch Rodel. Renish Point, the southern most point of Harris, forms the southern shore of Loch Rodel. Rodel was the focus of Alexander Macleod's eighteenth century scheme to develop South Harris. He built the harbour and the Rodel Hotel. An engraving by William Daniel in 1819 shows the layout of the buildings almost exactly as they are today. The exact date the hotel was built appears unknown. It has recently been refurbished and is now a modern oasis. St Clement's Church stands on a grassy hill with rocky outcrops overlooking the hotel and harbour.

St Clement's Church (Tur Chliamain)

The ancient church of St Clement's was the spiritual end of my journey through Lewis and Harris. It is the southern equivalent to St Moloug's at Eoropie. It is thought to be dedicated to St Clement's, Bishop of Dunblane from

1258–1266. The door closed with a clunk similar to that at St Moloug's leaving me inside the silent simple emptiness of this church with no furnishings. The floor is of simple glazed red tiles and the walls and transepts contain Macleod family tombs dating back to the mid-Sixteenth century. After my journey through Lewis and Harris this was, indeed, a fitting conclusion.

The church was built in 1528 by Alasdair MacLeod of Dunvegan and Harris. Alan McQuarrie, in his history of Cille Bharra, makes the point that hitherto it was fashionable for Celtic chiefs to be buried at Iona but in the early sixteenth century local burial in their ancestral home had become popular. John Griffiths, in the Pesvner Guide to the Highlands and Islands, declares St Clement's "the grandest Medieval building in the Western Isles." He describes the sixteenth century monuments of the Chiefs of the Clan Macleod as "the most impressive such collection in the Highlands and Islands." Each tomb is ornate. One has effigies of saints. There are four Celtic sword stones in the north transept. A tomb-stone in the north transept bears the initials RC MNS 1725. Another stone depicts the crucifixion and has a Celtic design on the other side.

The Reformation of 1560 is said to have marked the end of regular worship in this church. However Jim Crawford told me that he believed it had never functioned as a church. Rather it was built as a sarcophagus for the Macleod tombs.

The church yard contains a number of walled or railed graves, some overgrown with fuchsias. One stone caught my eye. It was inscribed:

K Macleod Deckhand RNR 4219/SD
HMS Vivid III.

18 September 1916 Aged 22.
Cha n'eil e marbh ach na chodail

The stillness of the church caused my thoughts to pause and I began to feel timeless, as if I could wait here for ever. I felt a calmness I had rarely before felt. My old life had just ended. A new life on different foundations had begun. The moment was precious. There was no hurry for the ferry at Leverburgh. I had time. There would always be another ferry. Life dictated not ferry times. Progress is only just if it is self directed exploration. Otherwise it is a treadmill. The quest for progress allows us to entertain the notion that we have better control of time but for most people it is, in fact, an illusion. The silence of the church induced a strong vision of self determination for myself and, if called, for others. Philippians 4 v. 8 came to mind:

> All that is true, all that is noble, all that is just and pure, all that is loveable and attractive, whatever is excellent and admirable – fill your thoughts with these things.

Also the words of the Hindu philosopher Tagore:

> Ever in my life have I sought thee with my songs.
> It was they who led me from door to door, and with them have I felt about me, searching and touching my world.
> It was my songs that taught me the lessons I ever learnt; they showed me secret paths, they brought before my sight many a star on the horizon of my heart.
> They guided me all the day long to the mysteries of

the country of pleasure and pain and, at last, to what palace have they brought me in the evening at the end of my journey?

Secret paths had taken me door to door in Harris. Maybe I hadn't seen everything in the island but I had gained rare insight. I had looked through the window in time.

When the time came to move on, it was no more than four miles to Leverburgh and the ferry to Berneray. The road went down between brown stone walls past some fuchsias and an old corrugated iron building. I passed an old barn with stone steps up to a large green door on the first floor. Then I saw a brown tourist sign in Gaelic and English which announced the beginning of the track to Borrisdale "Gu Borghasdal 1 mile".

At first it was a double asphalt track with grass in the middle along the side of a loch. It went through a five barred gate and over a wooden bridge then up and round the side of the spur Druim Sgeilechreac. This gave a good view over Rodel and Renish Point. Three rams, all with magnificent horns, looked down from a promontory above the track. After a short distance I had to climb over a narrow metal gate. The gate was jammed by massive stones on either side. The path continued through an old stone wall about three feet high overgrown with turf and heather which stretched down the foreshore. It swept down and round a small valley before climbing to Borrisdale along a magnificent angled stone embankment. In the valley at the foot of the embankment I saw a small structure with a bent metal roof which I took to be the cover to a spring, presumably once used as one of the village's water supplies. It reminded me of the spring which once supplied water to the Hostel at Rhenigidale. In Borrisdale the path lead across the drive of a modern bungalow and, thanks to two stiles, went straight across the well tendered garden of a house before reaching the road.

The road to Leverburgh from Borrisdale runs along the side of the hill overlooking the wonderful panorama of the Sound of Harris and its islands including the most notable, Berneray. The ferry was still a long way off. Finally the modern buildings of the quay came into view.

As I drank my tea in the Anchor Restaurant I reflected on my journey through the islands. I had walked just under 130 miles from the Butt of Lewis. The route had been easier to find than I had expected. Much, more than I had expected, had been over tracks and ways well defined on the ground. It made me believe that a linear long distance path through Lewis and Harris was possible. The Harris Walkway had shown what could be done with imagination and a little funding.

I had wonderful memories of Harris and Lewis: people driving past, smiling and waving; a bike leaning up against a wall (I bet it was unlocked and still there hours, maybe days, later); a red telephone box in the midst of the wild, its light on, (how welcoming it seemed); rabbits ambling across the road ahead. That steel grey uncertain dawn at Tong had blossomed into a beautiful golden sunset at Garenin and now the ebbing blue dusk of the Sound of Harris. My heart was full to bursting. I would never forget these islands.

Chapter 8

BERNERAY AND NORTH UIST: THE NEW HORIZON

BERNERAY IS THE island of my heart and always will be. It has everything – a wonderful warm community, a viable economy based on fishing, crofting and tourism, two shops, walks, spectacular beaches, thatched houses and a harbour that is the home of several inshore boats that fish for crabs, prawns and lobsters. There is a community hall with a lively programme of cèilidhs and events capped by a happy-go-lucky summer festival called 'Berneray Week.' This includes a curry night and ends with 'It's a knock-out' Eddy Waring style. Berneray is always such a happy place to visit. The Hostel is an integral part of the community, as it should be.

I first visited the island in 1978 with Petra, my wife, the year after the Hostel opened. We camped in the dunes near the Hostel but used its kitchen to cook our meals then in a large porch made of corrugated iron at the front of the thatched house. 1978 was also the first year in which the twins, Annie and Jessie, were wardens. By then I was engaged in a correspondence with Frank Martin the Hebrides Secretary of the Gatliff Trust. Frank invited me to become a Trustee in 1980. Progressively during the 1980s the Trust improved and extended the Hostel. It is now a popular refuge for travellers on their way through the islands. The first Annual General meeting of the Gatliff Hebridean Hostels Trust was held at the Hostel in 1989.

Berneray Hostel's location at 'Town' (Baile) on the island's east beach is spectacular. It is a wide expanse of beautiful golden sand starting just beyond a band of black rock that runs from the front of the Hostel into the Sound of Harris. The Sound and all the seas around Berneray are dotted with rocks of varying sizes each of which has a descriptive Gaelic name.

On clear days, to the east the panorama stretches beyond the Minch and the cliffs of northern Skye. On very clear days the mountains of the mainland beyond become the backdrop. To the north east the coast of South Harris is fringed by flat uninhabited islands. The mountains of South Harris, Ceapabhal, Grèabhal and Roineabhal, can be see through the gap between Ceapabhal and Grèabhal Beinn Rà, the peak on Taransay is visible. The tower of Rodel Church stands out on its hill, a carpet of green beneath Roineabhal, dappled by fleeting sunshine.

I sat in front of the Hostel in perfect peace watching the waves run up and down across the rocks. A broad spit of sand and rocks runs from just in front of the Hostel into the Sound. The passage of time and the outside world quickly become of no concern. This is the spirit of this place, its tranquillity and harmony stills the mind. A visit to Berneray always leaves me a long afterglow of clarity and vitality.

One September night, back in 1985, I sat here under the stars watching the Northern Lights, the Aura Borealis. A shower of diamonds splashed into the sky directly above my head. It was as if I was at the bottom of a deep sea watching sea shells disintegrating on the surface and falling towards me. Many years later I saw it again in North Uist. This time

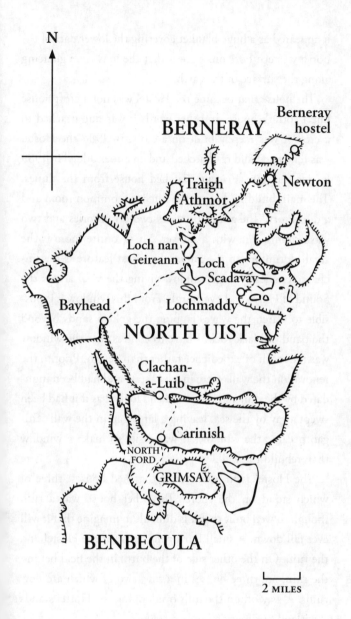

Figure 8   Berneray, North Uist and the North Ford

it appeared as a huge blanket covering the lower part of the north western horizon. I guess that the ions were glancing along the surface of the earth.

The house that became the Hostel was not a croft house but a cotter's house. In other words it was not attached to a croft it was merely built on a croft. In 1984 the Hostel was renovated and re-thatched and an annex added in 1989 by rescuing an adjacent thatched house from the dunes. The main building houses the kitchen, common room and a dormitory. The annex provides two dormitories and two wash rooms, one with a shower. My favourite room is the small dormitory in the annex. Its nicest feature is the un-characteristically large window giving the view across the Sound of Harris to Leverburgh. From this window it is possible to watch the waves lapping the golden sands beyond the band of black rock. I have to confess that the window was the result of expedience rather than design. Prior to the renovation the walls were in a bad state and had been inundated by the dune. The seaward end looked as if it had been swept away by the sea, leaving a large gap in the wall. This gap became the window. It was easier to make a window than rebuild the wall.

The Hostel is in a cluster of thatched houses, three of which stood on the shore. The other house was a ruin though so well built that it is difficult to imagine that it will ever fall down. A small burn runs between the Hostel and the ruin. On the other side of the burn, in the field behind the ruin, are three houses in a row, two of which are now ruins. A way off on the hills overlooking the Hostel stands the island's primary school.

The principle group of houses at Town includes a two storey stone building called 'The Gunnery of the Macleods'. The gunnery is a fortified building said to date back to the sixteen century. It was the birthplace of Sir Norman Macleod (1614–1705). This event is marked by an inscribed marble slab above the door. Norman Macleod was given his Knighthood for remaining loyal to the Royal House of Stuart. The Gunnery is, undoubtedly, a building of great antiquity though I always feel that the building next to it, a single storey thatched building, is older and more interesting. It does not look like a traditional island thatched house. Its gable end gives it a more Highland, Argyll, look.

The island of Berneray is dominated by three low hills, Beinn Shléibhe (93 m), Cnoc Bhuirgh (85 m) and Beinn a'Claidh (circa 35 m). The main settlements are at Borve, which lies along a valley between Cnoc Bhuirgh and Beinn a'Claidh and around the harbour and the bay, (Loch a Bhàigh) and at Ruisgarry scattered along the strand above the east beach. This is the site of the Telford church now unroofed and the Telford manse. These churches and manses were part of a gift to the Church of Scotland to celebrate the winning of the Napoleonic wars but quickly rejected by most of the local population.

A circular walk on Berneray

Walking around the island is a fine experience, well worth a day's pause in my north to south walk. I walked along the east beach to the end of the bay, about a mile, and climbed through the dunes to gain the headland. A road flanks the dunes alongside which patches of blown sand have overwhelmed the cropped grass. I walked past the end house of Ruisgarry and round the side of the hill, Beinn Shléibhe. The view over the Sound of Harris was spectacular.

The Sound between Berneray and Harris is used by a wide variety of marine and bird life as a thoroughfare between the Atlantic and the Minch and it gives access to the mainland. In most seasons there is a fly past of gannets from St Kilda, said to be the largest gannet colony in the world. These huge white birds, with black wing tips and sleek yellow bills and head markings, make quick time in flight. When looking for fish they wheel above a spot, diving only when they are certain of a catch. The dive is swift and deadly. The bird checks its flight, rakes its wings parallel to the body and dives into the sea. When they reappear on the surface, they can rise into the air after a few moments. Starting with a hesitant splashing of the water with their wings they soon rise clear to resume their majestic flight.

I climbed Beinn Shlébhe and sat by the triangulation point. To the north the Sound was picturesque. I could see over the small island of Killergaray to Leverburgh. Roineabhal bulked large. To the south I looked over Berneray to the northern shore of North Uist. Beyond, to the south, Eval, and North and South Lee dominate the eastern side of North Uist. Closer, just south of Berneray, I could see Beinn Aulasaragigh (217 m), Marieabhal (250 m) and Marrogh. To the west of Berneray is the island of Pabbay home to a huge herd of deer. Pabbay is a large island rising to a conical point (Beinn á Charnain). Two people are said to stay on the island intermittently but otherwise it is uninhabited. I remember a visit to Pabbay many years ago during Berneray week. The sight of a village of black houses inundated by sand dunes was moving. To the south of Pabbay is the smaller uninhabited island, Boreray, cut almost in two by a large loch (Loch Mór). Some Berneray folk are descended from the people who depopulated Boreray in the nineteenth century.

Immediately beneath me lay the west beach of Berneray, a large machair area and Loch Bhrusda. Machair is common throughout Uist. It is an area of grass created by blown sea sand. In spring and summer hundreds of delicate wild flowers and grasses perfume the air.

I descended Beinn Shléibhe and walked along the beach. After about a mile it bends more directly south west and stretches on for another two miles. It was totally empty of people. A breeze came off the sea. I walked along admiring the patterns in the sand picking up small pink shells and coloured stones. I looked across to Pabbay. After the turn Boreray came into full view. Prince Charles walked along this beach with Selina Scott in the 1991 TV film *A Prince in the Islands*. Why did HRH choose to be so vague and woolly during this scene? Sure Berneray is a place where outsiders come to dream but we can have a dream without appearing to be dreamers.

At the southern end of the beach is a headland, Rubha Bhoisnis, Braighe na Ceilp. From there I walked across the high grassed dunes to the cemetery. During my first visit to the island I admired the neat dignity of the place. Now as then some graves are marked with memorials of dried and plastic flowers under glass domes. On the way to the cemetery I passed the memorial erected in 1991 to Giant MacAskill of Nova Scotia. Angus Mor MacAskill stood 7 foot 9 inches high and weighed 425 pounds. 'Mor' is Gaelic for big. He emigrated to Nova Scotia in 1831.

I walked to the shore of Loch Bhurigh, a tidal inlet which resembles a mouth. The sands are completely dry at low tide and offer a short cut to Aird-na Rubhe close to the causeway to North Uist. A cable crosses the Loch from Aird na Rubha and is marked by a line of stones visible at low tide. Alongside the loch is a beached boat, an old landing craft once used for bringing cars and tractors to the island before it had a car ferry. I did not walk to Aird-na Rubhe but instead went along the machair to the Community Centre.

This took me past the site of the legendary Berneray Week 'It's a Knockout' and through Borve, past Burnside Croft. This is a working croft and guest house run by Berneray's most respected couple, Splash and Gloria MacKillip. Then I walked along the road around the bay, past the home of the Hostel warden, Alison. She is a woman of many talents, who has been known to drive the community bus, run the summer café at the Community Centre and work as a voluntary fire-fighter. I stopped off at the harbour to watch the fishermen off loading their creels and stacking crates full of velvet crabs on the quayside.

Further around the bay I came to Quay. On the shore is a cluster of old thatched houses, all but two in a bad state of repair. In recent years someone has renovated the houses nearest the school for a dwelling. On my first visit in 1978 the ferry was a wooden hulled boat plying to and from Newton Jetty. Passengers sat on deck. I remember a flock of sheep in the hull beneath. This boat is beached in front of one of the six old thatched houses.

Back at the Hostel I sat down to admire the view across the Sound. My walk round the island had covered just over 9½ miles. I sat in front of the Hostel enjoying the soft sunshine of a summer evening pondering, reading a book and chewing the fat with other hostellers, dream of the love of my life, wishing she were not so far away, watering the flowers on the window sill. Berneray is so other worldly. It is soothing to know that Berneray Hostel exists, is part of such a lovely community, a home from home for hostellers, a safe haven. Berneray is a community complete in itself constantly refreshed by the flux of people moving through the islands. The Hostel facilities are fit for purpose cherished by many from all over the world.

Berneray is no longer an island. In 1999 the causeway to

North Uist was opened by Prince Charles on a cold driech day. The event is commemorated by a stone at the ferry terminal. This change has not diminished the island's charms. If anything the vehicle ferry service to Harris has left the island more isolated because many people by-pass it.

To resume my walk through the islands I took the causeway to North Uist. As I crossed I watched the sea lapping its huge stones. On my walk to the causeway many people waved good bye, others passed friendly remarks through open car windows. I stopped at Ardmaree Stores for refreshment. From the causeway the Hostel looked small on the far south eastern point of the island. The car ferry arrived from Harris. Cars streamed along the swish new road before joining the single track road to Trumisgarry on the North Uist Circular Road. The waiting line of cars clanked aboard and the ferry set sail. A small bus left with its passengers. I arrived in North Uist.

North Uist

North Uist is a roughly square shaped island the bulkier northern section of which is ringed by a road known locally as the 'Circular Road' serving the bulk of the island's scattered townships. All other roads feed to the Circular Road. A large moor dotted with lochs occupies the centre of the island. The north of the moor is marked by a line of hills. North Uist's better known, more spectacular hills, North and South Lee and Eval (347 m), lie to the east along the Minch south from Lochmaddy.

North Uist is the gentle giant of the Hebrides. "Uist" is a funny sounding name for a delightful soft gentle place, an archipelago of islands large and small stretching from North Uist to Eriskay. Benbecula, Grimsay and South Uist are the principle inhabited islands in the chain. "Uist" derives from a Viking name. In the old days it was written as "Vist." It bears comparison to the name Unst in the Shetland Islands.

An old network of tracks was obvious in Benbecula and South Uist but North Uist was a puzzle. A Gaelic legend predicted the downfall of North Uist when it was encircled in black and a round house was built. By common consent the island was encircled in black in 1939 when the council finished layng tar on the Circular Road in 1939. A round house was built in 1958 by the then new owner of the island, Earl Granville. Fortunately the 'downfall' of North Uist has not yet occurred.

My plan was to walk from the Berneray causeway to the Circular Road along the machair which fringes Newton Ferry township thus avoiding the single track road which provides the four mile road link. I would then cross the moor in the centre of the island by the most expedient route before going down the south west coast from Bayhead to Clachan. The geography of the island pulls the route to the west as it crosses the smaller southern part of the island. The southern part is almost cut off from the northern part by a large loch, Loch Euphort. The loch stretches six miles inland from the Minch and almost touches a deep inlet from the Atlantic, Loch Oban a Chaechain. The distance between the two is no more than two hundred metres. This narrow corridor deflects the Circular Road to the west at Clachan. The road from Lochmaddy completes the circle at Clachan by joining the road from Solas and Bayhead.

This westward pull took my route away from Lochmaddy, North Uist's main settlement, which was a pity. In its day Lochmaddy has been Uist's main administrative centre with court, hospital, bank, and ferry terminal. Today it is enlivened by an imaginative arts centre and museum,

Taigh Chearsabhagh (nominated for the Gulbenkian Prize for Museum of the Year in 2005). Since the mid-1970s, however, Balivanich in Benbecula has been the centre of Uist. This is the location of the airport, the local authority's offices, hospital, shops and the military HQ.

From the Berneray causeway I walked along the road around a small hill, Beinn á Chaolais, to the junction with the local road (B893) from Newton Ferry. From here the B893 goes to the Circular Road four miles to the south west. After the rugged hills of Harris the wide open vistas of Uist are easier on the eye. The view to the south east is dominated by Beinn Mhór, the craggy glinting Beinn Bhreac to its north and Leathbhal to its south. Machair lays to the north west of these hills. The hills Crògearraidh Mor, Crògearraidh Beag and Maari fringing the North Uist Moor provided the southern skyline.

As the road goes round the base of Beinn á Chaolais it meets the sea on a low rocky cliff about twenty feet above the water, scattered rocks provide a home for seals. The houses of Newton cluster about the far shore of the bay. The top of the bay has a wide expanse of sand exposed at low tide with saltings beyond and a soft grassy sward used by the occasional camper.

Just before the junction, the road nears Loch an Sticir with its island Dun. The remains of Am Sticir are extensive, atmospheric, and linked to the shore by a stepping stone causeway. It is the site of a gruesome episode in North Uist history. This is where Hugh MacDonald, son of Archibald "the clerk", was seized in 1601 or 1602. He was later thrown into a dungeon in Duntulm Castle, Skye, where he was fed on salt beef and left to die an agonising death from thirst. The dungeon at Dunvegan Castle gives some idea of the barbaric conditions MacDonald must have faced. There the dungeon is a deep hole in the rock covered by a grill close enough to the dining room for starving prisoners to smell the food being enjoyed by the castle occupants.

From the junction with the B893 I could see across a field to a gate beside a green agricultural building on the south side of the hill Sudhananis. I walked to the building along the field boundary across the hump of a residual wall. I crossed the enclosure which included the building and made my way to the seaward fringe of Newton machair.

I chose to walk around the bay between the dunes. At this point the dunes are in parallel rows. Strictly speaking the area between the dune is the 'machair' but the term is applied more widely. A lot of marram grass was growing in the area. Walking along the beach took me to the headland called Hòrnais, at the southern end of the bay. I climbed the hill and from there could see the old burial ground and the more modern Clachan Sands cemetery alongside. Its approach road ran south west before turning south east to rejoin the B893.

I wanted to see an ancient cross. This involved a short detour from my route but it was worth it. It is a simple but well crafted cross with two limbs on the face of a large rock. Green and grey lichen made it difficult to spot though the rock is obvious enough. It looks like a glacial erratic, in other words it has just been dumped in the middle of a flat area. Erskine Beveridge calls it *Crois an t-Sagairt* and says it may mark one of the parochial boundaries of St Columba's parish of Sand. This parish dates back to at least 1505. He describes it as "a Latin Cross, ornamented by terminal knobs upon its top and arms and with a 2 inch spike stone as descending from its broadened base." He gives the measurements as 15½" by 11¼" and calls it a "cross fitché".

I continued on my way along a track from the bend in

the cemetery approach road. This took me alongside a field past a large agricultural building to a quiet road which also ran back to the B893. It went along the northern shore of a large sandy inlet. Nearby is a renovated thatched house let as a holiday cottage. This supports my theory that more of these houses can be rescued.

From the junction I had a choice of routes. I could have returned to the B893 and used it to reach the Circular Road about half a mile further south but I had realised that there was an alternative route to the northern shore of North Uist across the sands Tràigh Athmòr. I chose to cross the sands as it would shorten the distance I had to walk. I learned that the Gaelic name of the sands implies a ford.

As at Tong Sands I planned my crossing carefully. I consulted the tide tables published weekly in the *Stornoway Gazette*. The *Gazette* is widely available in the islands and though the predictions are principally for Stornoway, the table gives an adjustment for the time at Lochmaddy. A further adjustment is needed for Tràigh Athmòr. As at Tong the sands are dry for four to five hours.

I was clear about the line of my route and aimed to stick to it. I was advised not to deviate north as the sands shift and quick sands can be created. The principal danger I found, however, was that the sand is cut by deep channels with steep sides. Some were dry but others enclosed pools of deep water three or four feet below the surface of the strand. The most unnerving aspect is that the surface of the strand looks unbroken from a distance before the channel.

To reach the sands I turned south west at the junction. At the turn someone had created a small vegetable patch. I walked along the increasingly grassy pebble track through two gates. From the second gate the track went through the field as two indented ruts but I could see that I needed to strike more directly south south west. The foreshore was obscured by the hump of the grassy field created on the grassed over sand dunes.

I gained access to the sands through a gate and down a steep track. The sands are just under a mile across but distance is deceptive on the sands. Everything seemed so flat and the land appears elevated. It is clear from the black tide marks on the rocky shore that high tide brings three to four feet of water. A well kept Telford manse stands on the Trumisgarry peninsula next to an unroofed Telford church. Beyond the lumped summit of Crògearraidh Mor dominates the southern horizon. It looks like a volcanic plug left from an eroded volcano.

It is possible to come ashore on the Circular Road alongside a modern detached house clearly visible on the shore. However, I decided to cross the Cleit peninsular and gain access to shore at Geireann Mill or from Cnoc Mhic Eoghainn, the headland beyond. I struck south twice crossing the channel of a burn flowing across the sands. The burn was between ten and fifteen feet wide in both places but it was only a few inches deep, I could see its bed.

The peninsula is a fertile hump with lush grass divided into fields used by stock. The remains of old houses and stone enclosures can be seen on the western slope. Once beyond the modern fence, which is reinforced by an electric fence, I found myself on a wide grassy area above the foreshore. I walked a little way and went on to the sands through a wide gap in the flat rocks. The gap was wide enough for a boat or a tractor and looked natural, so large were the rocks. Maybe it was used as a small harbour.

At first I had to cross a rather slippery area of mud topped sand. Close to the far shore I encountered the first of the deep channels. To avoid it I kept to the sands but had to

scramble across rocks. The idea that I might cross the headland Cnoc Mhic Eoghainn was ruled out by another deep
channel formed by the outfall from Geireann Loch. So I
made landfall at Geireann Mill a mile from Grenitote. As I
left the sands I aligned my route with the conical hill Marrogh as its peak makes a good land mark from the sands.

If I had come ashore directly off Tràigh Athmòr by the
modern detached house I would have been half a mile from
Geireann Mill but this would have allowed me to walk past
Loch Aonghas with its fine reeds. From the road it is possible to see a dun in the loch with a massive harbour.

The old mill buildings of Geireann Mill have disappeared. The building at the site, which may have been part
of the mill complex, is used as a base for fishing parties.
I believe this Mill was more like the Breasclete and Gress
Mills than the Norse mill I had seen near Tolsta Chaolais.

As I walked along the undulating Circular Road from
Geireann it was impossible to miss a small cairn overlooking the road. This is a memorial to Mr John T Marcroft
FRCS, a surgeon from Greenock who visited Uist for fishing holidays. A little further on I passed a roughly hewn
milestone about six inches thick on the side of the road. It
stands two feet high with flattened top. This type of stone
lays in direct line of descent from the marker stones I had
seen on the way to Kinlochresort.

Just before Grenitote a large circular device has been
erected to commemorate 100 years of crofting in the township. From here a township road climbs up on to the moor.
I used this road to gain access to the centre of the island.
The track rose gently from the memorial went over a ridge
and dropped down into a hollow to cross a burn. After the
ridge the fences and agricultural activities of Grenitote were
out of sight. I found myself walking along the side of the

extreme north west arm of Loch nan Geireann. Its shore-line was obscured by a large reed bed. To the west was the slope of Beinn Dubh Sholais. The well made track crossed the burns by slab bridges and, after about a mile and a half, petered out at a small hummock. I was now in a wide ba-sin which ended on the shore of Loch nan Geirann. The basin was bounded to the south by the conical Marrogh and the Beinn Aulasaraigh hills which I planned to climb to get the view. I walked to the shore of Loch nan Geirann and continued south towards Skealtraval by the straightest route I could find, given the indented shore of the loch. Skealtraval is a low pointed hill with dense heather on its southern slopes.

I came to an artificially raised ridge covered with heather about two feet wide linking Loch nan Geireann to Loch Scadavay at a point where the two lochs come closest to-gether. This is an estate boundary at least two hundred years old. It would have cut the island in two, east and west. Most exciting, it is made of turf which confirms its antiq-uity. Turf was commonly used as a building material for dwellings and walls in the highlands and islands in the sev-enteenth and eighteen century. In walls layers of turf would be interleaved between stones.

In the nineteenth century it is said that Loch nan Gei-rann and Loch Scadavay formed an important north-south highway by rowing boat. Scadavay is nearly five miles long from north to south. In the south it almost touches the northern shores of Loch Euphort. In the north Loch nan Geirann is just over two miles from north to south and ends close to the northern shore of the island. The long shore-line and many inlets of both lochs, like extending fingers, combine to provide multiple routes across the island. It was common-place for people to use different boats in each loch but a boat might be carried across if it was light.

Today the southern extent of Loch Scadavay is cut by
the embankments of both the old and the new roads from
Lochmaddy to Clachan-a-Luib (known locally simply as
Clachan) which blurs the perception of the Loch as a north-
south route. The roads cross at a point where the loch is only
some seven or eight metres wide.

I walked along the northern shore of Loch Scadavay,
jumped across a substantial burn and settled on the shore
where another large burn entered the loch. Nearby was a
sandy beach which, I guess, was created artificially to assist the salmon. A large herd of deer looked down from the
upper slopes of Marrogh. A couple of Pomeranian skuas
flew around me. I remembered these aggressive birds from
Shetland so hoped they would give me a wide berth. As I
walked towards Marrogh a huge shadow fell across me. I
looked up and saw two golden eagles circling low. It felt
like a scene from a western film where the hero is limping
across a desert and vultures are waiting for him to drop. In
my case the eagles continued to circle but higher and higher
above the eastern slope of Marrogh.

To gain a vantage point I chose a gently ascending route
round the hill. The cliff on its southern face came into full
view. Beneath is a large chambered cairn, the twin of the
better known Barpa Langass. The Barpa is clearly visible on
a hill on the southern side of this basin, a couple of miles
away. Beveridge says the barpa beneath Marrogh is 60 feet
in diameter and reaches a height of 16 feet.

It was now a beautiful day, so still that I could hear the
flies buzzing around. Modern myth always associates Scotland with carnivorous midges. They may be troublesome in
parts of the mainland but I have rarely been troubled in the
islands. They were not in evidence today. The sun, however

148

had burned my cheek. I stopped on the slope of Marrogh, rubbed in some Nivea cream and drank some water. A herd of deer, almost indistinguishable from their surroundings, slowly ambled across the flat moor dotted with lochans (small lochs).

I climbed to the pass which separated Marrogh from the spur of Beinn had h-Aire and up again to the summit of Beinn had h-Aire. On some days Uist is hemmed in by mist, rain and cloud. Today the blinds were up and the panoramas vivid, both of the gentle island landscape and the wider southern horizon of the Inner Hebrides. A few clouds hung over the hills of Harris to the north. Berneray, Pabbay and Boreray were all clearly visible. Pabbay was distinct with its more pointed peak. So too was the much lower Boreray. But it was the view south which took my breath away. For the first time I could see all down the island chain to Barra. I could also see the hills of Mull with Coll and Tiree in the foreground. Way off to the south, feint, I could see the Paps of Jura. A few puffy clouds hung over the Cuillins on Skye to the east. The Atlantic sparkled.

Since leaving the Butt the Minch had been the dominant maritime influence on my route. From now on the Atlantic would dominate. This dominance emphasises the position of the Outer Hebrides as the north-west frontier of Western Europe. The Atlantic seaboard of Europe was once an important north-south corridor of trade, pilgrimage and ideas. Much of the islands' history can be explained by influences from the west perhaps more so than influences from the east. North-south influences tend to be Celtic or Viking. Eastern influences tended to be modern, anglicising influences. Figures revered in literature, for example Dean Monroe, Johnson and Boswell came from the east. (Monroe got to the Outer Isles; Johnson and Boswell only got as far as

Dunvegan Castle on Skye on their trip to 'the Hebrides'.) St Columba came from the south.

Does this help to explain the pull of the west, the New World, for islanders seeking a new life? It often amuses me to think that New York is a possible landfall on the other side of this vast ocean. In fact New York is further south. Hebridean shores are washed by the Gulf Stream. This is the tempering influence which gives these islands their remarkably mild climate. New York freezes in the winter; the islands rarely get snow.

Transatlantic aeroplanes cross the island every day on their Great Circle routes to North America leaving silent vapour trails in the sky. Another world away, the magic of flight contrasts with the stillness of the moor. Up there I imagine passengers enjoying their drinks, meals and on-board movies. Down here birds, perhaps ringed plovers, were making haunting piping noises. Delicate tormentils and pansies lay in the heather with cotton grass in abundance.

There are a series of inshore islands off North Uist, the largest and closest of which is Kirkibost and Baleshare. From Beinn had h-Aire it is obvious these two islands were a chain of sand dunes. They were detached from North Uist in a fierce storm during medieval times. Beyond this chain are the Monach (or Hesiker) islands seven miles off the coast and Haskeir which is eight miles off Griminish Point.

As I reached the summit of Marrival, the highest hill in this spinal chain, just as I hoped, St Kilda came into view due west over 40 miles away. It was a wonderful moment. The saucer shaped Hirta is the larger of the two islands. It swoops down to Village Bay and then swings up to another cliff. Boreray, to the north, is a chunky conical peak with two conical outliers. It looks like a medieval castle, two turrets flanking a central tower.

St Kilda is the ultimate untouchable Hebridean ideal, the representation of a way of life so isolated that self government was via its own 'Parliament'. The island was depopulated in 1930 but since the 1960s it has been occupied by army units who service the radar station which supports the Rocket Range in South Uist.

The distant western horizon stayed fixed before me as I mounted the last summit, Ben Aulasary. To the north, the island of Valley came into view. I stopped to wonder about this island. Here is another island of myth. Vallay is detached from northern coast of North Uist but it can be reached by walking or driving across the sands at low tide. The tide stays out long enough to allow time to explore the island. This tidal ford is still shown on contemporary OS maps and I have never heard it described as dangerous.

Erskine Beveridge built a substantial house on the island during the early part of the twentieth century. Today it lies gashed and forlorn, part open to the skies. Despite this, its modern grandeur is apparent. It looks like a detached suburban house, though larger. It is grey and looks larger than life, resembling the backdrop from a Hammer horror film.

Erskine Beveridge (1851–1920) was a linen manufacturer from Dunfermline. He had a reputation as a historian and biographer. In Dunfermline he was a local councillor, Chairman of the Hospital Committee, a Justice of the Peace and an Honorary Sheriff Substitute but was said to have "no taste" for the "controversies of local government". He was a Fellow of the Royal Society of Edinburgh and an Honorary Doctor of Laws at the University of St Andrews. It would appear from his obituaries that Beveridge was firmly rooted in Dunfermline. On North Uist the contemporary view is that Vallay was his home.

In 1901 Beveridge privately published a book about the

ancient duns or forts of Coll and Tiree. In 1897 he visited North Uist to compare his evidence from Coll and Tiree. Arriving in Lochmaddy he confessed to an adverse initial reaction caused by "the vast expanse of bogs occupying its east side, which is absolutely treeless and relieved only by a few hills of no great elevation and by the tortuous recesses of salt water lochs penetrating its seaboard". But as he got to know the island he was beguiled by its charms.

His great work *North Uist* was privately published in 1911. The book presents a comprehensive history and archaeological record of the island which remains unequalled. For many years the 350 copies of book printed lay hidden in libraries or closely guarded in private hands but in 1999 a facsimile edition was published (followed by a facsimile edition of *Coll and Tiree*).

I descended from Beinn Aulasaraigh to go round the southern slope of Beinn à Charra to look for a west-east track to Bayhead. I believed I would find its start on the southern slope of Beinn à Charra. To reach this point I fixed my line of sight on a chambered cairn, jumped a fence and walked across the springy heather to Beinn à Charra. The heather gave way to a soft sward. I crossed another fence. At first there was no track but it developed. By the time I reached the Committee Road the track was distinct. A fair sized stone stands on the westward facing spur which probably accounts for the name Beinn à Charra. In Gaelic this means the "Hill of the Rock." Beveridge records that the stone was 9 feet 3 inches above the soil, 6 foot 9 inches at the base and 5 foot 9 inches at the top. (Today the stone is lower because it has tilted.) He ascribes no meaning or purpose to the stone but I believe it is a navigational marker.

The summit rock of Creag Hastin, a mile to the east of Bayhead is visible some three miles away. This is aptly described by Beveridge as "a peculiar isolated rock somewhat resembling a ruined castle when seen from a distance". The Creag served as the venue for open air communions during the North Uist religious revival of 1957/58.

Much of the west side of North Uist is visible from Beinn à Charra. Kirkibost Island is distinct with its high dunes. So too is the Westford Inn solid and square with its central chimney stack. The homes of Bayhead were scattered about in the fields with the school and other homes in straight lines at the top of the bay. The area is overlooked by South Clettraval topped by a radar dome and aerials, including the TV transmitter. The line of sight between Beinn à Charra and Creag Hastin gave an almost perfect alignment with the track I was about to use.

To reach the beginning of the track I crossed a fenced field on the other side of the Committee Road. The track around the side of Beinn à Charra met the Committee Road directly opposite this gate. I found another gate on the opposite corner of the field which gave me access to the beach of Loch a' Charra. From here I picked up the track. It traversed a broad band of grass. At points it seemed to be floating on the surface of the peaty moor, at other times below the water logged surface. The track went to the shores of Loch Horisay. From there the track went between parallel burns to the shore of a small loch and on towards Bayhead across common land.

I crossed the burn which drained the small loch and walked along the Claddach Chnoc a Lin common grazings through a narrow gap between two fences both croft boundaries. These common grazings form a narrow wedge shaped piece of land which stretches to the foreshore. It is crossed by the A865, the Circular Road. Just before the Circular Road I passed a small windowless stone building with a rusty corrugated iron roof. This was once the home of the communal bull.

I crossed the Circular Road and made my way to the foreshore. Here is another ford. The channel closest to the shore is always full of water. The tide was coming so the channel was wider than at low tide. I had no need to cross to continue my journey because I was now going to turn south to Clachan. Nearby is the Bayhead shop, a useful and well provisioned stop for the long distance walker. It was originally the school serving children of all ages in this area. At Bayhead, I had walked just over 20 miles from Berneray Hostel, and called it a day.

The track from Beinn à Charra demonstrates routes that pre-date the present pattern of modern roads. Even after the construction of the Committee Road it remained the shortest route from Bayhead, Paible, to the moor and township peat cuttings.

The Circular Road, or at least the section running around the west and north coast from Clachan, appears to be an old way overlain by the macadamed road. One exception was the Committee Road. Its name gives the clue to its artificial origin. Beveridge says that it was a "relief work during the potato famine about the year 1846". It goes from the mill at Ardheisker to Malacleit township near Solas and Vallay Strand cutting the north-west corner of the Circular Road from the route.

Ardheisker is an area of scant population but in 1846 its link with Heisker, or the Monach islands as they are now more commonly known, might have given it more significance. (Heisker should not be confused with the rocky Haskeir which lays eight miles off Griminish Point.) The five Monach islands were populated until the early twentieth century, since when they have been used for grazing animals. Ard Heisker was their point of communication with North Uist.

Bayhead and all the townships along the west coast have a wonderful view over the sea but the view north is cut off by a line of hills from Beinn Ernaigeitir in the east to South Clettraval and beyond to Carra Crom. (Possibly another residual volcanic plug) The township of Balmartin beneath Carra Crom was the scene of a land raid as recently as 1951. Just to the south of Balmartin is Loch Hosta. Hosta machair is the scene of the annual North Uist Agricultural Show, Highland Games and sheep dog trials. Reclaimed fields on the south facing slope of South Clettraval give the hill a patchy look. Balmartin was not the only land raid in North Uist. A land raid also took place at Balranald in 1920/21. This is commemorated by a recently erected standing stone on the Circular Road just south of Kilmure Church. As a result of the raid Balranald was acquired by the Board of Agriculture in 1922. Part of this area is managed as a nature reserve by the Royal Society for the Protection of Birds. There are complaints by crofters about the rapid increase in population of migratory geese which visit the area.

The route to Clachan was a puzzle. The now asphalt road was the natural route, in fact it looked like the only route. Its antiquity is emphasised by the up-ended stones which line parts of it. Despite that, it did not present an appealing prospect. It is an undulating single track road with no footway. The coastline, a shoreline with many inlets, presented an alternative route. Most boundary fences and walls stop well short of the foreshore leaving a wide area for walking.

From the ford at the end of the Claddach Chnoc a Lin common grazings I turned south and walked past the ruins of large thatched houses close to the shore. One ruin presented a wall fifty yards long. It seemed to be two or three houses in a row. These ruins reveal the old pattern of settlement with its dual dependence on sea and croft. The old houses faced the shore well away from the road.

As I came adjacent to the gap between Kirkibost island and Kyles Paible on North Uist the sea was frothed by the on-shore wind. If it was not for Kirkibost and Baleshare island off the coast the waves would have been more troublesome. The high dunes of Kirkibost were impressive.

The three houses at Ardheisker, came into view. The thatched house at Ardheisker once had two thatched byres. The inlet just north of Ardheisker was flooded so I had to walk up to the road. At low tide it would have been possible to cross and go around Ardheisker before regaining the road and across the causeway in front of Ardheisker. Just before the inlet I passed a huge metal drum standing on the foreshore. It resembled a huge oil drum on its side about five feet high and ten feet wide with mooring rings around its side. This was the largest piece of flotsam I was to encounter. Apparently the drum has been on the foreshore for years. (It disappeared during the great storm of January 2005.) I had already passed a milk crate from Miami, a sheep's skull and four metal balls used as net floats.

The causeway at Ardheisker divides the tidal saltings from the rest of the inlet which now forms a large loch. The road sweeps round a huge black rock, its northern face cut by a 18 inch wide band of white rock. I returned to the shoreline past the house on the southern side of the inlet. Its outhouses were once used as a mill. Two large grind-stones lay in the grass.

Once again the shore took me south across headlands, round inlets, one with stepping stones. South of Ardheisker the inlets were not troublesome so I made quick progress. The tide was receding. The biggest delight was that I was well away from the road. I continued to amuse myself with the flotsam: a fish box from the Foyle Fisherman's Co-operative, plastic bottles of all shapes, sizes and colours, bits of tree trunk, a milk crate from Remington Farms New Jersey, plastic and metal net buoys and dozens of glass whisky bottles. I passed the backs of houses, some with buildings near the shore to support small fishing boats. Bits of old tractors and other agricultural machinery lay here and there. Oyster catchers flew noisily along the shore. Lying in one inlet I saw a big old wooden boat about 30 feet long and 10 feet wide. Later I passed an old landing craft which looked as if it might be submerged at high tide, then an old rowing boat, its rowlocks still in place.

There is a large standing stone, Clach Mhor a Che, 'great stone of the world', on the shore behind the Westford Inn. According to Beveridge it is "supposed" to mark the site of a battle. I passed the back of the old school at Claddach Kirkibost, now being used for an imaginative community centre. The cafe provides a wonderful view over the inlet.

The shore continued to get closer to the road until they joined. I managed to get round without getting my feet too wet. I walked the last mile and a half to Clachan along the road and passed the Hebridean Smokehouse in a new large purpose built building. I have always enjoyed their peat smoked local salmon. At the top of the hill just before the Smokehouse there is a small memorial cairn commemorating the first landing in the islands by the Air Ambulance Service in 1933. The plane landed on the sands beneath this hill at low tide.

At Clachan the road from Bayhead joins the road from Lochmaddy and continues south to Carinish and Benbecula. It crosses a bridge over the tidal inlet Oban a Chaechain before undulating to Carinish alternating between single and double tracks. Because of this I was not keen to use it. Instead I passed Clachan stores at the junction and walked the half mile north east along the Lochmaddy road, the A867, to the Locheport turn. I walked along the deserted Locheport road to a southward track across the moors. The road took me past the old pier which used to be visited by Clyde puffers. An agricultural co-operative has on and off occupied the old pier building. Beyond, on the northern shore of Loch Euphort is Langass Lodge, a smart hotel. It looked stately amongst the trees.

Just beyond the inlet Oban na Curra, the track south rose up from the road to a gate. I crossed the subsequent field to a fence. As I hopped over the fence I got a fine view to the north of Roineabhal in Harris. The view east was dominated by North and South Lee and to the south east by Eval. All the hills looked splendid, on their best behaviour, their grey rocks catching the sun. From the fence I aligned myself between two cairns to the south on the north west side of Craonabhal, the "crown hill". Beveridge says they are chambered cairns. I crossed a field of short grass and heather. Just before getting to the cairns I switched from OS 1:50000 Map 18 to Map 22. This is the penultimate map of the Outer Hebridean series.

Loch an Iasgaich (the 'fishing loch'?) lay ahead beyond another fence. The map showed a narrow neck of land be-tween Loch an Iasgaich and a larger unnamed loch. Near the crossing point is a small hump of a hill, like a lump. The crossing, however, was not as it seemed from the map. It was not two lochs joined by a burn but one loch with a wide channel between its two parts. This was a blow. Some large stones in the channel tempted me to cross. They were hardly stepping stones, there was a significant gap in the middle. So I had to jump. I made it, just. (A walk to the west around the loch's shore might be a safer alternative.)

The moor continued on the southern shore of the loch. Another pointed hill lay just ahead. I passed two small lochs, climbed the hill and looked south. I could see Carinish township clustered on the edge of the moor. Rueval on Benbecula was clear to the south. I continued south past the end of Loch an Droma and Loch nan Clach and picked up a pebble based township track. This wound around the moor seemingly to take advantage of the rock outcrops. It took me to the building, with three circular holes for ventilation, just opposite the Carinish Inn which used to be a cow shed. A similar building once stood on the opposite side of the road but this was demolished during the hotel improvements in 1999. It had been the stable for two horses used to draw a trap to convey people across the ford.

I was now at the start of the walk across the North Ford. Carinish lays astride the A865 road but part of the township is on a bulbous headland. This is the site of the battle of Carinish and the Teampull na Trionard, the Temple of the Holy Trinity. The Temple is said to have been built about 1200 by Bethag daughter of Somerled, Lord of the Isles, the first Prioress of Iona. It is thought that Robert the Bruce spent some time at the Temple in 1306-7 whilst in exile. It was a significant centre for learning and teaching. Sadly the Temple is neglected and some walls look in danger of collapse. There is a good view of the Temple from the lounge of the aptly named Temple View Hotel.

The battle of Carinish took place in 1601. This involved a small group of MacDonalds of Sleat and North Uist who defeated a larger 'raiding party' of Macleods of Dunvegan and Harris. Few other details are known.

I had walked about 13 miles from Bayhead. I was now 33 miles south of Berneray Hostel.

Chapter 9

THE NORTH FORD AND BENBECULA

I HAD HOPED for bright sunshine for my 5½ mile walk across the tidal sands from North Uist to Benbecula but it was a typical grey Hebridean day. Known locally as the North Ford, the actual ford is simply a channel near the northern shore of Benbecula. Crossing the North Ford alone was a supreme experience. However, I undertook the crossing with care.

The road which has, since 1960, linked North Uist with Benbecula is about a mile longer and uses a series of causeways, small islands and bridges. It is a single track road without a footway and in places runs between high stone walls. This makes it an unpleasant, if not dangerous, walk. I had, however, been warned of the dangers of crossing the North Ford just as I had been warned of the dangers of using the ford across Tong Sands.

Mindful of these warnings the first time I crossed the Ford, I was guided by Mr Ewen Nicholson of Grimsay. Mr Nicholson and his father were guides who took people across the Ford before the Causeway opened. People travelling from North Uist would linger at the Carinish Inn to wait for the tide. There were other landfalls in North Uist. For example one is directly beyond the Post Office at Carinish. Post was brought directly from the airport, which is just across the bay, on foot and by boat. I made the second crossing alone using Mr Nicholson's directions. I found it easier to cross with Mr Nicholson, but common sense, caution, a compass and a willingness to correct mistakes got me though on my own.

I walked down the track from the Inn to the sands. I had checked the tide tables in the *Stornoway Gazette* and made the necessary adjustment from the datum to the Ford. The inlet, Bàgh Mòr, reaches inland about half a mile to Carinish and is dry for 4 or 5 hours at low tide. It takes about an hour and a half to make the crossing. Bàgh Mòr opens on to the sands of Oitir Mhò, I kept close to the shore to avoid a channel from the sea, Struthan na Comaraig, which reaches close to Bàgh Mòr. I passed the point Aird nan Sruban, which marked the first mile, and took a line on a shed with a red roof on the island of Grimsay. From the map, especially any OS map published before the Causeway, the crossing looks straight-forward but from the sands the route is not so easy to find. At sea level everything looks flat. The brown/yellow sands bulk large. Water caught in the sand ripples glistens in the sun. Reassuringly the foreshore, and the islands ahead, are close. A band of islands lays across the sands. The road on its causeway is also obvious from the sands, close enough to provide a fall back.

Just to the south of Aird na Sruban, close to the shore of North Uist, the first line of the 'Mackay stones' came into view. These navigational markers present a line of rocks a foot or two apart. Their age and history is unknown. Mr Nicholson told me that the lines used to be more extensive. In places they gave an almost complete line across the open sands to prevent travellers getting lost or drowning in channels where the water was too deep. Seton Gordon com-

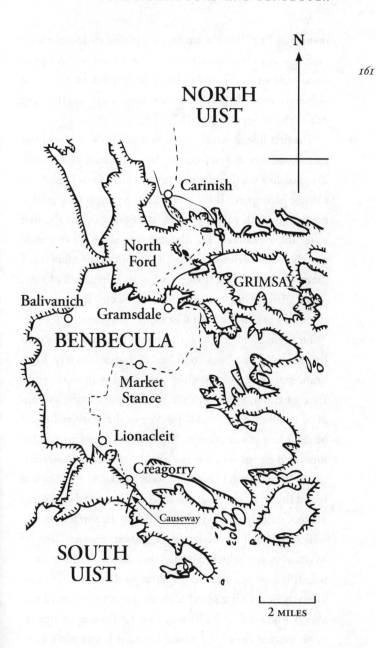

Figure 9 The North Ford and Benbecula

mented in 1927 that the stones were placed in position after an Excise man was lost on the Ford. He went on, "A line of stones was set in the ford to keep the traveller on track and although some of these stones are sunk deep into the sand others can be seen distinctly."

The first line of Mackay stones was a little scattered but each stone was distinct despite being covered in seaweed. The next line was longer with nearly thirty stones neatly set a single pace apart. This line about thirty yards long guided me to the south east towards a safe spot to cross the first water filled channel. The channel was about 15 feet wide and the water between 12" to 18" deep. On the other side I found the next line of stones, with a new alignment of 190°, which directed me towards the south west. The way went through a gap in the 'island of shells', Caigionn.

From the sands the islands present themselves as a continuous band but I was confident of finding the way. I had heard stories of sinking sands associated with the islands. I accepted that sands do shift but felt that so long as I applied common sense and kept close to the markers I could be confident of safe passage. Mr Nicholson advised me that some of the gaps through the islands were difficult to navigate. On my second crossing I went too far to the east and found this to be the case. The sand was loose and sticky and my foot quickly sank a foot or so below the surface.

Before reaching Caigionn I passed another line of Mackay stones which directed me across another channel. This took me close to the shore of the island Grimsay. Grimsay Post Office stood high on the nearby shore. I had always wondered why Grimsay Post Office was on this remote western tip of the island but now it was obvious its location facilitated the receipt of the mail from Benbecula. The line of stones ended in a "T". The cross piece pointed the route to Grimsay.

At this point, I found it necessary to re-align my bearing to find the correct gap between the islands. A bearing of 220° brought me to Caigionn. I could see a small island topped by a pyramidal grey rock. To its east is another, smaller, island with the foundations of a large cairn on the summit. The gap through the islands, known as "Dorus na Caigionn", Door of the Caigionn, is behind the cairn.

Dorus na Caigionn lay on an alignment of 300°. It is a wide gap with a basin. In the basin I picked up a short line of stones which bent to the right (west). Looking back I got a fine impression of the whole curved line of stones. I had seen such curved lines in old photographs.

I kept in the middle of the basin but it was a little slushy. Despite this I had no fear of sinking. Just ahead I came upon a ten foot wide track through the rocks bounded on either side by raised stones. The marks of tractor tyres were visible along the track. Mr Nicholson told me that the RAF had cleared and widened this way during the war to facilitate passage by their lorries to the observation post on the western end of the Caigionn islands. They erected the stones on either side of the track to stop their drivers going astray. The red-brick buildings of the former observation post now stand roofless some distance away.

When I emerged from the islands I found I was aligned with the sand dunes at the north eastern end of Benbecula Airport, under the flight path to the main runway. I crossed another short slushy area and then went through another widened track before emerging on to the wide strand known as Oitir Mhòr. The North Ford is a channel on the northern side of Oitir Mhòr.

There are no Mackay stones on Oitir Mhòr. Instead navigation was facilitated by three large cairns each about ten feet high. Today only the middle cairn of the three is still standing. (Sadly it was swept away in the great storm of January 2005.) The other two, like that just north of Dorus na Caigoinn have been demolished. Travellers aligned the first cairn with the other two to take them straight across Oitir Mhòr and on to the North Ford at the correct point. I had passed the base of the southern-most of the three cairns at the end of the track through the island of shells. This was about twelve feet across and looked as if it was on top of a small island. I found that the correct alignment from this point was 240°. An alignment with the distinctive inverted conical water tower in Balivanich is unhelpful as it is on a bearing of 260° from this point. Nearby on the islands of shells is a tall yellow diamond sign showing where the power cable goes underwater. It is now near the causeway. This spot also fails to provide the correct alignment.

It was about a mile across Oitir Mhòr to the North Ford. The sand was firm all the way but I had to avoid one or two pools. I did have to cross one small channel. The large sea channel Beul an Toim between Baleshare and Benbecula is sharply defined by the dunes on either side. As I crossed the sands the view of the channel opened and closed as the headland of Aird Mhòr, Carinish and the Eilean Lochdrach, the western most of the Caigionn islands, became the shutters.

At last I came to the North Ford itself. It lays in a deep channel with a slightly humped bank, close to the northern shore of the island of Benbecula. Though the channel always contains water the width narrows at the lowest tide. If the walker finds that the water is flush with the top of the bank the Ford would be too deep to cross. In those conditions, walk to the Causeway and go over the bridge.

I chose to cross the Ford at a spot where there was a band

of rock on the northern side, and one or two rocks on the southern side. Its width varied, but here it was about twenty feet across. The water went up to my knees. The sand on each bank was wet and loose but this did not present a problem.

As on the North Uist side there was a choice of landfall on the Benbecula side dependant on the traveller's ultimate destination. People wishing to travel north from Benbecula could wait for the tide at the Gramsdale Inn, a temperance Inn near the main road south of Market Stance. A horse and trap was provided from the white house next to the Gramsdale Inn. I wanted to continue on a more easterly route towards Flodda so chose the most easterly of the landfalls. This is close to the twin tone brown fish processing factory at Gramsdale.

I came ashore at the end of a track alongside a small green hut and a smaller unpainted wooden hut. This is also where the telephone cable comes ashore. The spot is marked by another yellow diamond sign. By now it was a sunny day, though a little chill, with blue skies and puffy clouds. I was glad to be ashore, safe and sound. It had taken me about 1½ hours to cross.

Benbecula

Benbecula is about a third of the size of North Uist. It is perceived as the bustling administrative centre of the southern isles but by southern standards is quiet. Balivanich, the island's main town, looks positively suburban thanks to small estates of ex- Ministry of Defence housing. However, two thirds of the island is uninhabited moor. This lies to the west of the A865 the inter-island north-south road. It is a wide, open, low wilderness with many lochs with one major hill Ruabhal (124 m). The B892 loops through Balivanich from the A865 at Gramsdale and re-joins it just north of Cregorry.

Benbecula's airfield played an important part in the Battle of the Atlantic. The predecessor of British Airways had flown from Sollas in North Uist but this service was transferred to Benbecula after the war. In 1958 Balivanich became the Headquarters of the Royal Artillery Rocket Range. I imagine that Balivanich is the township in the Uists most often encountered by English people through the experiences of military postings. (The pop singer Miss Dynamite spent some time there during her youth.) I wondered about the impression it gave of the islands. Some love it stay or buy second homes. I fear, however, that many hate it and may have conveyed their negative impressions to their friends back home. The winter storms and the fresh summer breezes which come off the Atlantic are not for everyone. If the wind was too strong at times, I hope when it dropped they heard the true song of the Hebrides in their hearts.

The distinctive inverted conical water tower in Balivanich remains in view from many parts of the island. Directly opposite is MacGillivray's, a gift shop, also selling clothing and intriguingly it has the best collection of second hand books on the Islands and Scottish topics. I regretted not visiting Balavanich as I always find a trip to MacGillivray's rewarding. I would have taken the opportunity to visit Maclean's bakery en route; their award winning light bread and Scottish Parliamentary oatcakes are memorable.

The track from the shore took me back to the A865 just after its landfall on Benbecula. I wanted to sample the island's remote eastern moor and from there walk to Market Stance in the middle of the island, just west of Ruabhal. This would avoid using a long stretch of the A865. From Market Stance a network of old tracks still exists. I was confident I could find an acceptable route along these tracks south to Lionacleit.

I walked a short distance south down the A865 to the turn to Kyles Flodda. The sun was shining on Eval as I turned east along the road to the island of Flodda. This road skirted the northern coast of Benbecula. About half a mile from the turn is another recently renovated thatched house let as a holiday cottage. I passed some modern cottages built on either side of the road and turned south across the moor just before the causeway to Flodda.

I followed the shoreline. To the south of the causeway is a large inlet. I did not expect to find any markers let alone a track across this part of the moor. Tantalisingly, however, just off the road, I saw a pole on the moor. Three grouse flew up from the heather almost under my feet which gave me a fright. I soon came to a large sandy bay which I crossed maintaining my line of sight on Ruieval. On the other side of the inlet, on Flodda island, there was a small building with a slate roof obviously formerly a thatched building.

This line took me to a ridge overlooking Loch na Bèirè on which I found the remains of two thatched houses. I assumed that people walked house to house across the moor, as I could see no fixed track. As I gained the top of the ridge a fantastic view of the three peaks of South Uist opened to the south. Macleod's Tables in Skye were also clear to the east. To the north a bigger surprise: I could still see the hills of Harris. I walked along the side of Loch na Bèirè with its island covered with scrubby bushes. I climbed another low hill, having crossed the line of a couple of fences just to the north of two small lochs, the wires long since disintegrated. From here I could see the east to west track which would take me west to Market Stance. According to Ray Burnett this was the Clanranalds' kelp road.

I joined the track just before it crossed an embankment between the two lochs, Loch na Deighe fo Thuath to the north and Loch na Deighe fo Dheas to the south. (Thuath means north, Dheas south.) Beneath the embankment were some low bushes. Water flowed between the lochs through a culvert under the track. The track went through a gate in a fence and passed the northern slope of Ruieval. I resisted the temptation to climb to the summit. Instead I found a flat rock and sat down for a coffee from my flask. The view was fantastic. The islands' blinds were up again. To the south I thought I could see the Paps of Jura and beyond them the hills of Argyll. The water tank on the rocket range on South Uist was silhouetted against the sky. Closer, on Benbecula, Griminish Church was prominent across the hummocky moor with its many lochs.

The track took me past the sheltered Loch Bá Una. Innumerable gulls occupied the loch just a short flight from the local authority dump at Market Stance. A big dumper truck was working up and down on top of the rubbish. This disturbed the birds on the dump and caused them to wheel about in a huge screeching cloud. The track rose to the level of the dump bringing the huge red local authority building at Market Stance into view. I walked to the building and crossed the main road.

Market Stance is elevated and gives fine views across the island of Benbecula towards Aird, Balivanich and the Atlantic in the west and to the south. Lionacleit school, the Dark Island Hotel and just beyond the wind turbine in the dunes were all visible. Golden sunshine burst over the sea.

Beyond the cross-road I continued east and passed the modern water works owned by the Water Company, with its characteristic pagoda tiered top. I was back on a pebble based township track. From here I gained access to the network of tracks. The north-south tracks are neglected to-day but the east-west tracks have largely been overlaid with tarmac. The north south tracks would have been important before the road, the A865, crossed Loch Olabhat.

Loch Olabhat is a large narrow loch, over a mile long, which lays north west to south east across the island presented a barrier to north south travel. The A865 crosses Loch Olabhat at the point where the road is bordered by thorn bushes after which a brief vista of bushy islands in a loch opens on both sides of the road. In fact the road crosses two short causeways. Prior to their construction a long detour to the west would have been necessary.

I could see another track going directly south. I jumped the double fence at the gate, which had been used as a temporary sheep fank, crossed a field to a second gate and made my way along a wide well-made, but neglected track. This took me down the side of Loch nam Faolieann past peat cuttings and across a stream, where the surrounding ground was rather soggy.

At the southern end of a small loch I passed a derelict thatched house. The old track came to the road alongside a house. The last part of the track doubled as a drive to a garage at the rear of the house. I turned west towards Griminish township along the modern road. I passed a small red roofed house with a blue and red tractor and trailer in the yard. To the north, beyond a small estate of Council houses, was Loch Fada, a narrow loch with steep sides. Ahead I could see a telecommunications tower. It is a complicated affair with dishes and drums on three of its four sides and a low transmitter building. It stands adjacent to St Mary's Church and presbytery. But before I reached the mast I came to the track south to Torlum township.

At Torlum the track emerged at the old school after passing a small wood of coniferous trees growing through plastic tubes. This repeats the historic pattern of paths being built to get children to school. Torlum township presented a mixture of buildings including an old thatched house with bits of turf still hanging from its walls. A red and white hulled yacht lay in front of the house. A phone box completed the scene.

I turned east past the front of the old school and walked along the road to join the final track south. This would take me to Lionacleit across a stretch of land called Cnoc-na-Monadh. I passed several houses including one with diamond roof tiles, pastel green door and two sash windows and a renovated house with two doors, one marked 19. Houses are numbered according to the number of the croft on which they stand. Consequently the numbers do not necessarily run consecutively through the township. A house called "Willow Bank" had an attractive cultivated garden. A large peat stack stood behind the house opposite.

The track south was between a red roofed bungalow and a double storied black roofed house. It continued across the field between wire fences, crossed a stream by a stone bridge and traversed a soggy area. This took me to a better footpath across a field and eventually to a narrow wicket gate held shut by a wire. I emerged on to a track. Two houses stood at the top of the track. A line of washing hung outside one. A lad in a football strip, football in hand, stood at its gate. In the field an old bath provided a drinking trough for the animals, a common sight in the islands. It was a short distance south to Lionacleit along the track.

The temptation of a short detour to the Dark Island Hotel with its terracotta roof was great. Next to the Hotel the larger building is Lionacleit Secondary school which opened in the 1980s. The building also houses a library, museum, theatre, swimming pool and cafeteria all of which are open to the community.

I remembered *Beòshlaintean* – the Uist millennium exhibition which I had been held at the Museum. I echo the hope expressed by the audio visual *High Tides*:

> ... *Almost gone now the black houses of our ancestors* ... if only the traditional wisdom can be retained despite the tide of modern times, the islands will survive.

The road south to Cregorry was straight-forward. A footway runs alongside the B892 and then south along the A865 to Carnan Stores on the northern shore of South Uist. I walked past the guest houses of Lionacleit, the scatter of houses of Cregorry township and the Co-op. Just beyond the Co-op is a group of council houses called "Ford Terrace", another reminder of the old means of inter-island communication.

Chapter 10

SOUTH UIST AND ERISKAY

SOUTH UIST IS a gentle long lush island. A wide strip of beautiful soft machair fringed by dunes of variable height runs alongside the Atlantic, the west side of the island. The eastern horizon is dominated by mountains set in a wide moor. Of those mountains the three peaks Hecla (606 m), Beinn Corradail (537 m) and Beinn Mhor (620 m) provide a picture post card crescendo to the drama of South Uist's hills. Townships dot the machair from Iochdar in the north to Smeircleit in the south. In the middle is Howmore, a convenient and historic staging post with its thatched house Hostel. The influence of the Atlantic is constant from sea breezes, the noise of its pitch and swell and the smell of seaweed.

The A865 runs north south from Carnan to Daliburgh where it turns east to the ferry port of Lochboisdale. South of Daliburgh the north south road is continued by the B888. The line of the A865 & B888 divides the island into one third fertile machair and two thirds mountainous moors.

The historic road runs the length of South Uist from Carnan in the north to Ludag in the south. It is over 300 years old being shown on the map of Uist published in Blaeu's Atlas in 1662. From Carnan it runs along the north shore of South Uist to Cill Amhlaid from where it runs as a green machair track 23½ miles to the Pollachar Inn. Using this historic way I expected my walk through South Uist to present a gentle view through the window in time.

The South Uist machair and its many lochs offer a rich and varied habitat alive with wild life at all times of the year. The gentle grasses and flowers which perfume the spring and summer air give way in autumn to the waving marram grass on the dunes. The birds of the beach, foreshore, machair and lochs, tell the tale of the changing seasons. Uist is on a main north to south migration route for many species of geese and swans. From the air and on maps South Uist's lochs make the island look like a lace curtain. In the autumn large reed beds stand yellow and crisp on the shores of lochs.

To achieve its straight course the A865 crosses Loch Bee, in the north of South Uist, on a causeway about half a mile long. Loch Bee is vast. It is the largest brackish water loch in Scotland covering 7.1 square km. It is about 5½ miles long and a mile at its widest point. To the east of the road it narrows and contains a series of islands. It is famous for its colony of mute swans. Loch Bee is so extensive that it almost detaches the top, north eastern, strip of South Uist from the larger southern chunk.

Loch Bee must have presented a more substantial obstacle to north south transport than Loch Olabhat in Benbecula. Loch Olabhat was sufficiently narrow to permit reasonably quick passage by boat or even the construction of a make-shift bridge. Neither would have been expedient at Loch Bee. Once Loch Bee was crossed by a causeway there was no need for travellers to take the historical route. All the townships of South Uist are accessible from both the old and new roads. Most now run across the machair between

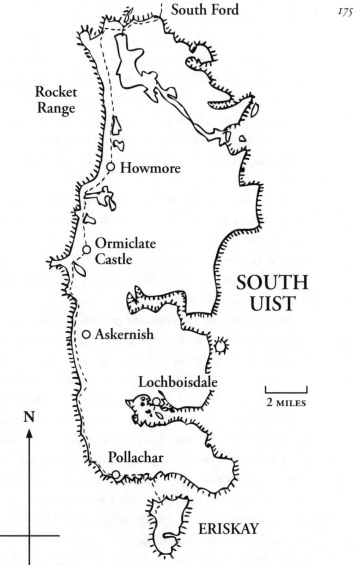

Figure 10   South Uist and Eriskay

the two. South of Daliburgh I imagine there was always a duplicate north south road from Lochboisdale to Pollachar. Daliburgh is the only township along the road.

South Uist and Benbecula were joined by a road bridge in 1939. Prior to this, passage between the two islands was across the mile wide sound by boat or across the sands at low tide. This is the South Ford. The old bridge was replaced in the 1980s by a modern Causeway built on a high rock embankment. The sands are exposed between Carnan, South Uist and Cregorry, Benbecula, for four or five hours a day.

I had heard so many stories of sinking sands or quick influx of the tides at the South Ford that I nearly avoided making the crossing. The adjacent Causeway offers an acceptable alternative. The road is double track and well surfaced, which encourages motorists to speed over, but there is a footway along its whole length.

The old road over the Causeway goes down to the shore adjacent to the car park of the Co-op store in Cregorry. When I arrived at the Co-op I found the tide out so I took my chance and walked the short distance to the foreshore. The Ford itself, the most significant of the channels, is on the Benbecula side. A wide pool greeted me, but the pool was narrower just beyond a large area of black rock. The water went up to my knees. Soon, however, I was back on firm dry sand which stretched all the way across to Carnan Stores. After a short walk on this line I was surprised to discover the circular base of an old marker cairn. It was quite unmistakable having seen similar ruins on the North Ford. Later I found a sketch of the South Ford which showed a cairn in a pamphlet by Wattie Nelson published by the Scottish Youth Hostels Association just after the war. However, the cairn appeared to be on the rock outcrop I had passed just before crossing the Ford. As I approached Carnan I had to cross two or three shallow braided channels. One had marker stones to guide the walker.

The ford makes landfall in South Uist adjacent to Carnan Stores, a builders merchants owned by the Iochdar Community Co-op. The track rises up from the sands on the western side of its wire fenced compound. This took me past a shed and yard supporting a fish farm business. A boat was high and dry in front of the shed.

The track touched the A865 at a cross-road of asphalt roads. The north to south legs are the A865. The eastern leg goes down to the shore but the other, going directly west, is the start of the old road to Cill Amhlaid. I turned along the old road and shortly after saw the pretty sight of a recently renovated thatched house near the shore. I believe this was the ferry man's cottage. By sad comparison there are many empty thatched houses, most with ragged and decaying thatch, scattered throughout the area.

The old road had been tarred until the last croft. Shortly after, the indented northern shore of South Uist came to meet the metalled track. Here the sound between South Uist and Benbecula is a wide expanse of sand at low tide. A sand spit, named Gulan, almost blocks the western end from the Atlantic. Across the sound the rotating blades of the wind generator at Linolcet School jutted above the swaying marram of the dunes. I passed the Hebridean Jewellery Workshop after which the track was, once again, tarmaced. The Workshop is a local enterprise which creates high quality jewellery based on modern interpretations of Celtic symbols.

The road crossed an inlet by a short causeway and rejoined the quiet local road. This took me all the way to the northern fence of the Rocket Range at Cill Amhlaid. I passed one of the area's glass fronted wayside shrines containing a statue of the Virgin and Child. The shrines are said to have been erected in the 1950s and are thought to be unique in the British Isles. They are common in some Catholic countries. This shrine stood on the Atlantic dune beyond which was a pretty bay.

The road crossed the northern tip of Loch Bee. The loch touches the road as if it was just another burn but beyond the 'burn' the Loch's wide expanse is visible. The main buildings of the Range clustered around its water tower on stilts are on the southern shore of the loch. The white painted Ardkenneth Church stands on the northern shore of the loch. It appears long and low because the church is joined to the Presbytery. Beyond, the southern sky was blue and yellow.

At the road junction just prior to the Range I came to a phone box and a glass-fronted notice board. This reports the state of firing on the Range. I had written to the Range Commander to seek permission to cross. He informed me that the old track was still a public right of way and that the land remained under crofting tenure. However no walking is permitted whilst the red flags are flying. These are hoisted half an hour before any firing. If the red flags are raised walkers have to leave the Range immediately. There is no firing on Sundays. I once saw Rapier surface to air missiles being fired on a grey cloudy November day. It was an awesome sight. Missiles streaked upwards into the clouds chasing remotely guided target aircraft followed by loud bangs.

I was in luck. No red flags were flying. I walked the short distance to the fence and went through a gate on to the Range. So far so good. Ahead was the flat green expanse of the site. The grass of the Range fronts the Atlantic for about four miles and has Loch Bee is on its eastern boundary.

The Rocket Range was created in 1958. It is one of only two ranges in the United Kingdom where the firing of live missiles is permitted. At the time local opinion was strongly opposed to the development but was placated by the Ministry of Defence's decision to open the NAAFI (Navy, Army, Airforce Institution) store in Balivanich to all. At that time its worldwide counterparts were only open to military personnel and their families. Compton MacKenzie used the story as the template for an amusing book, *Rockets Galore*. Written in the genre of his better known *Whisky Galore* the threat of a rocket range in the "Todday Islands" is seen off after rare pink seagulls are discovered. The rockets were not allowed to disturb the habitat of such unique birds.

In 1994 when the range was threatened with closure there was equally strong opposition. One local person, Seonag Campbell, was quoted by a Glasgow newspaper, *The Herald*, "I don't know how long we would keep two ferry terminals if the base closed and British Airways certainly wouldn't have a daily flight to Glasgow." 286 local jobs were said to be sustained indirectly by the base. The threat passed but sensitivities remain.

Though activity at the Range has been scaled down in recent years it remains one of the most visible reminders of the military presence on the islands. Less obtrusive are the huge runways at Benbecula and Stornoway airports. Radar domes and wireless aerials can be seen on various hills. South Clettraval in North Uist is the most visible.

As I crossed the Range I could see no evidence of the old road but the walk was straight-forward. This gave me time to admire the profusion of birds and flowers inhabiting the area. I doubt if there has ever been a track over this land, as old maps show the way petering out in this area. I fixed my line on Sheaval (223 m) a hill about 10½ miles to the south and reached the southern fence in just over an hour. My path south crossed the concrete base road just where it crosses a stream by a flat concrete bridge. To the left the base road reached the main gate. Its red and white pole barrier pole was up. The camp buildings looked deserted.

The old road started at the southern boundary of the Range as a pebble based track of considerable antiquity. From the southern boundary fence I could see Drimore Farm to the south east and beyond it the low hill Ruabha, a foothill in the South Uist range. The Range Control occupies the summit. Beneath it, on the slope facing the Atlantic, is Hew Lorrimer's statute of Our Lady of the Isles. Erected in 1958 it is tall, slim and white "in characteristic semi-naturalist manner" according to John Gifford. It reminds me of the Easter Island statues staring to the blue Pacific horizon.

In contrast to Drimore the next farm to the south, Grogarry Lodge, is surrounded by trees. The Lodge was used by the families of the syndicate which bought the South Uist Estate in 1962. The Estate covers over 90,000 acres mainly under crofting tenure and includes Benbecula and Eriskay. It is also said to be the biggest crofting estate in Scotland and is well known for its trout fishing and snipe shooting.

South of Drimore and Grogarry the mixed crofting economy became more evident. The machair soil is easy to work and the track passed many patches cultivated for arable and others with potatoes. Sheep and cattle were also in abundance. The walk to Howmore passed the townships of Grogarry, Stilligarry and Drimsdale. Each township seemed to be matched by a loch. The old road passed the lapping shores of Grogarry Loch and then crossed a wide burn by a wooden board bridge draining from the Loch to the sea via a small loch called Lòn Mòr. The boards sagged alarmingly as I crossed. Then the track petered out for a while before it passed the shores of Loch Stilligarry. A blue Ford Van rusted by the track, its doors ripped off. An agricultural building of semi-circular corrugated iron nestled in a fold in the dunes.

After Drimsdale the track was well defined. It climbed a low hill from which I got a good view of the broad sweep of the bay. To the north the Range pill boxes stood out on the dunes. I passed Loch an Eilean. The ruins of the island castle Bheagram were visible in the loch, its circular curtain wall evocative. Within the enclosure is said to be the foundations of a number of buildings including the main tower. This is thought to have been 12½ feet high. In 1505 it is known that Ronald Alensun, a relative of the Clanranalds, held it as a place of refuge rather than residence. Its subsequent history, like that of many other ancient and historic buildings in Uist, is unrecorded and therefore is ignored.

A hint of coal smoke greeted me as I approached Howmore township. The old road took me past the church before turning towards Howmore township and the Hostel. Howmore is a pretty township with several thatched houses in a variety of styles. One of the thatched houses is the Gatliff Hostel. At the seaward end of the township is an historic Church of Scotland. Its yellow wash and red streaked roof contrasts with the green of the machair. Its arched bell chamber facing east is empty but the gable facing the sea is topped by a weather vane. Inside the church has an unusual gated communion table running from pulpit to door. Church of Scotland Communions take place at defined times of the year after considerable prayer and preparation. Historically Howmore has always been a Protestant enclave in the predominantly Catholic South Uist.

Howmore is a place of considerably historical and ecclesiastical importance in Uist. It is draw in red on the map in Blaeu's Atlas. The early history of Howmore is undocumented but it is thought that the Christian settlement started with a small missionary cell in the sixth or seventh century. "How" comes from the Norse "Haugr" meaning a burial mound. Howmore's importance increased during the Lordship of the Isles and by 1505 the Clanranalds were well established in the area. Churches were seats of learning in medieval times. They brought together men whose general level of education was well above that of the ambient population. They were also the focus for pilgrimages either in their own right or as a stopping off point on the pilgrimage route through the islands. No wonder the medieval writer Cathal MacMhurich described the Hebrides as a "forest of learned men." This allusion to Howmore as a place of learning and hospitality pleases me as it fits well with the ethos of the Hostel.

The ecclesiastical ruins are close to the Hostel. This include an ancient church dedicated to St Mary and an equally ancient chapel dedicated to St Columba. A third chapel is said to have been removed by 1866. Howmore is said to have been the site of a parsonage belonging to the Abbot of Iona. The whole area is covered in burial mounds. It was from within these ruins that the Clanranald stone vanished in 1990. It is a stone commemorating the burial place of the Clanranalds and is thought to have been made in the sixteenth century. It was leaning against the wall of Caibeal Chlann ic Ailean, the highest and focal point of the burial mound. Fortunately the stone was found in a flat in London and returned to Uist in 1995. It is now the centre piece of the Kildonan museum. It is a pity that a replica has not been returned to Howmore.

The stone is a fine example of medieval heraldic art. According to the Royal Commission for Ancient and Historic Monuments in Scotland the arms show "in the dexter base a Lymphail with rudder, central mast and sail set, above is a hand couped bearing a wheel cross. In the sinister base is a castle and above a lion rampant; in the centre and surmounting the whole is a bird on a thistle slip". Soon after the stones return to South Uist it was realised that this description was incomplete. A fish was found on the lower part of the stone. It must have been obscured by the peat in the cemetery.

The Howmore Hostel stands between Howmore's contemporary and historic churches. It opened in 1966. Betty MacDonald, the current warden is the daughter of Mrs MacSween the first warden. She visits the Hostel on her bicycle. The Hostel is one of the few traditionally thatched houses in the islands still in use. A traditional thatched roof is local poetry because its method of construction and the materials used completely mesh with the materials the local area could provide at the time of construction. In 1984 the Gatliff Trust realised that it was possible to thatch on to a boarded and felt covered roof. Stuart Bagshaw had been responsible for renovating a thatched house in this style in Howmore village. This preserved the external appearance of the building but also gave a more water tight interior, a prerequisite for usage of electricity. Since then this style has been used at both Berneray and Garenin.

The Hostel was recently rethatched in authentic traditional style using heather because there were problems obtaining marram bent. This work was carried out in 2000 by Brian Wilson. Brian is known in Scotland for his trip by canoe around the coast of Scotland, immortalised in his book *Blazing Paddles*. When Brian removed the old roof he found that marram was the predominant thatching material but straw, rushes, iris leaves and water reed, heather and bracken had also been used. All the materials were laid on to a layer of turf without fixings but "an almost continuous stratum of hand-woven heather rope" was used. The roof timbers included a miscellany of items including an old oar.

Sitting outside the hostel overlooking Howmore bog is a fine experience. It is peaceful, sheltered, spot from which the corncrake can be heard in summer. The corncrake is a small brown bird which migrates to the United Kingdom from North Africa to breed. Now confined largely to the Outer Hebrides the male marks its territory and calls for its female partner by making a loud, persistent croaking noise. It is one of the wonders of nature to be found in the isles except when one is trying to sleep.

Howmore to Eriskay

The twenty mile walk from Howmore to Eriskay is easily achievable in a day. The causeway to Eriskay which opened in 2001 runs from Ludag, where the passenger ferry used to leave for Barra.

The day I left Howmore to go south massive clouds billowed into the infinite deep blue sky. The sky is always massive at Howmore. The view to the west across the Atlantic offers wonderful golden sunsets and the midnight sun in late June. I walked past the church to the old road, forked to the south and crossed the Howmore River by the well made concrete bridge. As I approached the bridge the wide estuary to the west opened between the dunes. Brown cows grazed nearby giving off a strong sweet smell of fresh grass. Was that a redshank running along the bank of the river towards the shore?

I walked along a stretch of modern road, passed Howbeg

to Stoneybridge. This is the only section of old road between Howmore and Pollachar Inn which is used by the current road network. On this 1½ mile stretch I only encountered the community minibus and the post van. I used the road but it was equally feasible to walk along the machair or an alternative track through the dunes. I passed a football pitch, the first of many in South Uist. Cows grazed on the pitch unconcerned by my passing. Swans dotted Loch Rog nearby. The south west wind had blown the clouds off the hills revealing the three magnificent peaks of the main hills of South Uist which overlook Howmore.

As the road swept back from the dunes towards Stoney-bridge the old road took a course more directly south and rose as an incised track to the top of a low hill. Just before the road made its turn away from the sea I passed a massive shingle bank blown or washed from the sea. Water had been trapped by the bank creating a small loch and a boggy area on either side of the road which was partly covered by large reed and iris beds. Just off the coast lay Varren Island, the island of the 'wild cabbage'.

At the summit of the low hill the track passed a deserted farm house. Its storm windows faced inland, two dark eyes viewing the landscape. A tractor pulling a trailer had climbed the hill from the south and its driver was now at the back of the house unloading bales. From the top of the hill I could see Ormiclate Castle, less than a mile away, set in a wide sweep of South Uist. The castle was my next goal. I walked down the hill to the flat machair passing a walled cemetery in the dunes, its neat monuments in lines, its gate posts each topped with a cross. I crossed a drain by a slab stone bridge. A blue tractor with a trailer came towards me from Ormiclate.

Ormiclate Castle is the ruined fortified home of the

MacDonalds of Clanranald. Built in 1701 it was destroyed by fire in 1715 and has been open to the sky ever since. It is surrounded by a nineteenth century agricultural steading. This gives it the appearance of a medieval village clustered around a great hall. The castle was larger than I had expected. Agricultural equipment lay around the steading in various states of use or dilapidation.

The map showed the old road going south from Ormiclate but on the ground it appeared to cross a cultivated field so I followed the field boundary. I could have used the road from Ormiclate to Bornish but did not as I was keen to investigate the old route as thoroughly as possible.

Once on Bornish's wide and green machair, with its line of linear lochs trapped by the dune, the track reappeared. Two huge skeines of geese flew along the machair in an elongated V shape. I reached the Bornish township road end. Bornish House and St Mary's Church dominated the township. The church is long and low, grey sided with a small campanile topped by a cross. As I continued south three swans flew along the machair eventually landing on Loch Bornish. Their graceful flight was matched by an imperfect landing. Just as the birds were about to land the wind lifted them slightly higher. One turned. The others seem prepared to go on but checked their turn and landed. Their hasty splash down was a wonderful sight.

The old road across Bornish machair lead to Kildonan township machair. Like Bornish machair it was wide and grassy and sloped gently up to the first ridge of a double dune which blocked all view of the sea. Way ahead I could see someone was working on a tractor but I could not hear the sound of the engine. A huge flock of waders rose high above me, uttering, twittering as they went. They turned with a great flash of silver/white diamonds sparkling briefly in the sun. I passed a large metal agricultural roller weighed down with rocks in fish boxes.

The map shows a standing stone on Kildonan machair but it has disappeared into sand. Rabbits were much in evidence as was a collection of rusty iron on the township dump in the dunes. Three curlews flew past. The track rounded a corner at the end of the Kildonan road. A low loader was parked by the roadside. There were also a few creels, lobster traps. In the township I could see two thatched houses.

The dune was replaced by a rocky shore on which sea-weed, kelp, was piled high. On the beach, amidst the kelp, were metal and plastic floats, bits of tree trunk, fish boxes, even a traffic cone. A dead seal lay on the sands. Shortly after I came across cows on the beach. I crossed the outflow from Loch Kildonan, one with a tongue of concrete running out into the sea.

To the east, across the loch with its reed beds, I could just make out the memorial at the birthplace of Flora Macdonald. Flora was the heroine who saved Bonny Prince Charlie from capture after Culluden by dressing him as her maid as they rowed from Uist to Skye. Described by Rosalind Marshall as "slim, dark and dignified", she was 24 years old, "well brought up, she was musical and she seemed intelligent, sensible and resourceful." Despite Flora's heroism Charles is said never again to have contacted her.

As Bornish machair merged into Milton machair the land became sub-divided into fenced plots. On top of the dune I found a well defined sandy track which took me to the Frobost road end. From the top of the dune I glimpsed the cleft in the hills between Barra's highest hill Heaval and its smaller companion Hartaval. Barra beckoned. It was a wonderful moment.

Ahead I could see Askernish House, for years the administrative base of the South Uist Estate. Cattle grazed among the dunes. Swans, ducks and geese swam on Loch na Liana Mòire. To the east I could see the hill Askervein (125 m) topped by a radio mast. In Askernish township there was a thatched house with a blue van at its door. A white car, an old plough, a rusty green lorry and an old tractor were scattered about the township.

Askernish machair is the home of South Uist's golf course. Its Club House is a wooden hut. A sign announced the green fees: Ladies £2.50, Gents £3.50, Juniors £2; Day ticket £5. A silver painted post box was proffered for their collection. Askernish machair is also the venue for the South Uist games in July. The games include athletics events, tug of war and Highland dancing. Much fun is had by all. On the day a flutter of vans and tents surround the circular sports field selling tea, burgers, chips and ice cream. There is even the odd travelling salesman peddling his wares, shoes or clothing, maybe books or china.

As I crossed Askernish machair an area of blown sand obliterated the track. Further south I could see a radio mast which I knew was adjacent to the track, so that became my aiming point. I came to a cultivated field crossed by the tracks of a wheeled vehicle. Afterwards the track climbed a hill past a walled cemetery. I rested a while with my back to the cemetery wall and enjoyed the view east across the machair. I could see the houses of Daliburgh in the distance at the junction of the A865 and B888 roads. The machair was full of lochs, some with reed beds like the nearby Loch Hallan. The moor seemed close, but the hills at this point are not as high as the three peaks overlooking Howmore.

I continued past the radio mast. The road to the cemetery gate turned sharp east and returned to the township but the old road continued south. I crossed the machair and

walked along the top of the dunes to avoid a strip of potatoes. Here I found the dunes lined with make shift fences
erected from whole tree trunks set on boxes. I imagine that
these logs arrived as flotsam. Had they escaped from timber
rafts at river estuaries in North or South America or had
they been washed off the decks of ships in storms? Shortly
after, I passed hundreds of pallets stacked in the cleft of
the dunes. Walking along the top of the dune gave views
across the open Atlantic. The ocean is so huge, so powerful.
Against it Uist seems so small, human, fragile. The huge
ocean lay under a massive sky.

The track divided. I took the leg down to Kipheder machair where a large herd of brown and white cows were grazing
alongside Loch á Gheàrraidh Dhuibh. Within the township
I could see the gaunt structure of an old church, its roof
open to the sky. A patch of sun slowly moved north over the
hills. As it passed over the top of Ben Kenneth, which overlooks Lochboisdale, the summit turned white in the sunshine. Ben Kenneth is the goal of a local race each August.
On the return leg to Lochboisdale competitors can either
run the whole way or swim the loch. In recent years winners
have all run the distance rather than swim the loch.

The track disappears for a short distance on Kipheder
machair as the ground is a little boggy. It reappeared shortly
before joining a road from North Boisdale. This took me
past the remains of scarecrows, an old plough, harrow, and
a roller. Fragments of plastic bags stuck to barbed wire blew
noisily in the breeze. Offshore the top of Orosay island appeared high compared to the terrain on South Uist. A factory building once used for processing seaweed into fertiliser
came into view. I passed North Boisdale cemetery clustered
in the dunes around a large ruin. I wondered if it was a family tomb or the ruins of a chapel. I could see the track ahead

winding its way though the machair grass. Some plots were cultivated and others fenced.

The walk across Garrynamonie machair took me to an inlet which I crossed by a small well made bridge. As I approached the bridge I thought I could see a wrecked boat amid the flotsam and jetsam. The 'boat' turned out to be the remains of a whale, its bone being about seven feet long and two and a half feet wide. Several other whale bones were scattered about.

Beyond the inlet the track divided. I choose to continue along the machair track rather than take to the dunes. The way improved. I passed an old man with a peaked cap and specs driving a cow. We exchanged greetings. It was the first time I had spoken since leaving Howmore Hostel. I crossed a slow flowing stream by a low flat board bridge and walked along the foreshore on a reasonable track. The beach to my right was covered in piles of kelp amidst which birds were piping. I passed a couple of smallish unroofed thatched houses and arrived at the southern shore of South Uist. An inviting yellow halo hung over the island of Barra across the sound.

I turned south east along the southern shore of South Uist to Ludag. I crossed a burn, Ceann á Gharaidh, flowing into the sea through an elaborate series of concrete channels enclosed at the seaward end by metal doors. I joined a road but left it shortly afterwards to take a track along a more direct route to the Inn along the top of the low earth cliff. I ended my walk to Pollachar Inn along the beach. Sweet yellow plants covered the rocks of the beach. The sea was blue, deep translucent blue.

I paused a while by the menhir in front of the Pollachar Inn. It must have provided a useful navigational aide. The Barra mail ferry once berthed at Pollachar Inn. Not surprisingly, therefore, the old road ends at Pollachar.

A track continued beyond the Inn car park so I did not have to walk north along the B888 to take the road to Ludag. I continued along the top of the low cliff around a neat modern house and field. At one point I had to hop over the fence into the field to avoid an eroded section of the cliff. An old fishing net lay on the beach below. Once on the road I walked the remaining distance to Ludag without too much interference from traffic. I was intrigued by a modern house enclosed by a high wall.

Eriskay

The modern causeway arcs across the sea to Eriskay. I camped above the Prince's Beach about a mile from the causeway and overlooking the new terminal. The area is also used as a golf course and is home of the "Eriskay Open". This is typical of the verve of some islanders.

Eriskay is famous for three things: Eriskay ponies, "Whisky Galore" and the fact that in 1745 it was Bonnie Prince Charlie's first landfall in Scotland, hence the "Prince's Beach". He is known to have stepped ashore on to a rock in the middle of the beach. In the dunes above the rock a cairn was erected in 1995 on the 250th Anniversary of his landing.

Eriskay is a small island about 2½ miles by 1¾ miles. Most of the houses are concentrated around the northern bay at Haun, where the causeway now arrives or around Acairseid Mhòr. Acairseid Mhòr, a bay which opens into the Minch, looks like an open mouth and divides the larger northern part of the island from the south lobe. The northern part of the island rises to Beinn Sclathan (185 m). South of Acairseid Mhòr the main hill is Beinn Stac (122 m). A short chain of smaller islands runs from the south of the island like a goatee beard on the chin of Eriskay. The largest island, Na Stacem Dubhas, has the bulky remains of a castle, Caisteal Ruebadair, on its summit. A good view of the castle is had from the ferry to Barra.

My day on Eriskay was wet as predicted by the radio weather forecast. I had first visited the island in 1983 and although I had a returned a few times, including 1995 for the commemoration of Bonnie Prince Charlie's landing, I had never explored the wild eastern side of the island. I particularly wanted to see if any remains of the SS Politician, the "Whisky Galore" boat were visible.

A few tracks showed on maps but none led far. All were clustered around the main settlements. The Tourist Board had published a leaflet about a circular walk around the inhabited western part of the island. Historical evidence, including maps, showed that people walked from house to house. In 1934 the German anthropologist Werner Kissling stayed on the island for six weeks and recorded many details about the way of life on the island. He made a film, *Eriskay. A poem of remote lives*, which caused a stir in London. Its Premier in 1935 was attended by the Prince of Wales. It showed people walking from house to house.

My day in Eriskay was grey but despite that I decided to try to walk around the island. I walked from the Prince's beach along the road to Haun and took a short track marked on the 1:50,000 map to the community co-op's grocery store. I found the track without difficulty as it was indented into the grass. It ran from the drive of two houses across a plank bridge over a burn and went up a slight rise to the back of the Co-homun's shop. The path obviously went to the school as this is directly opposite the shop.

I stopped outside the shop to make a note. A man with a dog asked if I was lost and I asked him about the track. He told me that the track I had just walked was easier to find this week than last as the weeds on the intervening ground had just been cut. After we said farewell he crossed the road and disappeared into the school playground.

I remained outside the shop trying to interpret the scene. A couple of women tourists clad head to foot in blue nylon walked past and went into the shop. An elderly man came out carrying his shopping in a plastic carrier bag. He too went through the school playground. Intrigued, I watched him emerge by a side gate. From that gate he seemed to be walking through the tall grass. I realised that I was witnessing house to house walking. I followed at a respectful distance. He was walking along a hardly perceptible track which wound its way across open land to his house. As I followed in his footsteps I could see many informal tracks crossing the open land at the crown of the hill in the middle of the township. My spine tingled with excitement, wet day or no.

I walked along one of these informal tracks towards the jetty. From there both a road and an old track went out towards Rosinish Point. It is here that the *SS Politician* sank on 5 February 1941. The boat sank with a cargo of at least 20,000 cases of whisky. The events that followed inspired Compton MacKenzie's book *Whisky Galore* published in 1947. In turn it inspired the popular phrase "Whisky à Go-Go" in the 1950s and 1960s, a phrase used as the name of many night-clubs. The film of the book, the first UK film to be filmed entirely on location, was shot on the Island of Barra.

I followed the track from the jetty past the front of a derelict cream painted house with red diamond tiles and side extension. Concrete utility posts appeared down this track. This is the 'old road' built with the proceeds from the

London premier of Werner Kissling's film in 1935. Paths went off to left and right.

There was a good view down to the Sound of Eriskay. In a field closer to the shore I glimpsed two white ponies – a mother and a foal. I crossed a bridge; one or two of its planks were missing. The track and the road crossed. The track passed an unroofed thatched house and after a gate narrowed to about four feet before going through a deep cleft between two rock cliffs. I could see to the Minch beyond the island of Hartamul, but Skye was invisible in the grey. Near the end of the track were several empty stone houses in various states of decay. An upturned boat lay by one, its red timber keel visible through the dying bracken. It brought to mind the house on Jura in which George Orwell wrote *1984*.

There was a good view of the island Calvay just off the coast of Eriskay. The tide was low and Calvay was almost joined to Eriskay by a crescent shaped sand spit. This is where the SS Politician went down. Nothing was visible.

The Sound of Eriskay is narrow at this point. The hills of the Glendale area of South Uist were clear on the other side. The highest peak is called Roineabhal. Interestingly its better known namesake in Harris stands in the similar proximity to the southern coast of that island.

When I first visited Eriskay in 1983 I was told about the 'Pipe Ski' in the Sound. It had made the national TV news and sounded hilarious. Eriskay's priest had water-skied up and down the Sound playing the bagpipes to raise funds for the church.

I walked south over the slope of Beinn Sclathan to the inlet Acairseid Mhór. This was straight-forward but there were some surprises. The landscape is one of ridges and valleys but several streams have cut deep gorges to the sea. Two appeared unexpectedly. In both cases I found myself suddenly looking over a rocky cliff.

There were water lilies on the small Loch Duvat. Shortly afterwards I came upon eight Eriskay ponies grazing with foals in the distance, the first of two groups I was to see. The Eriskay ponies are a recognised breed which live wild on the island. They looked so peaceful that I tried to pass quietly. They decided I was no threat and carried on grazing. The variety of colours, greys, blacks, browns and whites, made them almost invisible against the rocks.

I breasted the ridge overlooking Acairseid Mhór. In the bay was a yacht and two fishing boats. Two new houses on the south side completed the gay scene. The 1882 and 1904 maps show a track to Heisinish point but I could not see it on the ground. I could, however, see the walls of an old house. From it a track of sorts ran west. Perhaps this was a fragment of the old track. Having seen this track, maybe with the eye of faith, I could see the track to Heisinish going through a deep gorge just as illustrated on the old maps. I followed the track west from the old house. Like the tracks in Haun it wove its way through the ferns crossing the rocks, dips and burns. It took me to the head of the bay from which the road went back to Haun.

Before I got to the road I passed a traditional slate roofed house with storm windows all boarded. Its byre was made of corrugated iron and board, its roof weighed down by rocks and drift wood. A green hulled boat lay alongside. On the other side of the byre was a blackberry bush. Just beyond I crossed a plank bridge, adjacent to a modern blue and white mobile home and a collapsed netted thatched roof of a byre. Creels were stored inside an old mobile home.

Back on my first visit to the island the post box nearby declared "No next day delivery" with amusing candour. I walked north back to the Prince's beach past a huge iris bed and a house with a white sculpture of two horses in its front garden. This reminded me of the gate post sculptures of Ness. Next door was a renovated cottage with a Ballachulish slate roof. With the eye of faith I could see feint house to house tracks running between the houses scattered between the road and the Prince's Beach. I used one of these tracks to walk to the cairn above the Prince's Beach after crossing the new road to the ferry terminal. A lot of snails had found a home between the stones at the top of the cairn.

The visibility had improved since I left my tent in the morning and I could now see the northern shores of Barra. Later that evening I walked past two cemeteries to the Am Politician pub, bold with flags flying. En route I got good views of Pollachar Inn and Ludag. A happy end to a happy day.

Chapter 11

BARRA AND VATERSAY

AND SO FINALLY Barra. Barra is a small, roundish island, with a nose protruding northward towards South Uist. Barra's townships largely face the sea to the east. Like North Uist, it has a circular road but it is not referred to as such on the island. The island's central moor is mountainous rising to the peaks of Heaval, the highest, Hartaval and the twin peaks of Thatabhal. Castlebay, the island's main town, lies in a secluded bay facing south across to Vatersay. In 2004 the owner of the island, the MacNeil of Barra, gave it to its people.

The ferry took me to Ardmhór. I walked to the junction with the spinal road. At the junction I did not join the spinal road but went sharp right, past the phone box. This lesser used road took me down to the sands of the cockle shell beach Tràigh Mhór. The tide was out but I could see it was on the turn.

I crossed the sands from a slip alongside a house at the roadside and walked on to Eoligarry. The land rose gently from the dunes and crofts. I could see Cille Bharra within a walled cemetery on the hillside. I could also see the 1881 track going from the cemetery over the hill.

Cille Bharra is the ancient church of St Barr. Within its

walled enclosure are the ruins of Cille Bharra and the South Chapel. The North Chapel has been roofed. According to Fr. Calum MacNeil, writing in 1984, the instincts and oral traditions of "Barra people ... link them with Finnbarr of Cork and Brendan of Clonfert by way of Eilean I ("Iona")." Cille Bharra appears to have been in continuous use as a medieval parish church. The current ruin is thought to have been constructed in the twelfth century. Like the Macleods of Harris the MacNeils of Barra were probably buried on Iona but after the fourteenth century they were buried at Cille Bharra. The sixteenth century grave slabs preserved in the re-roofed North Chapel bear witness.

The Reformation of the mid-sixteenth century made little impact on Barra and within a hundred years Catholic missionaries had returned to the island. The MacNeils of Barra converted to Catholicism in 1632 and in the eighteenth century native priests trained overseas were replaced by missionaries.

Within the restored North Chapel an altar has been set up. It is a place of peace and tranquillity. I paused for a silent prayer of thanks for the success of my work, "guide my hand to do Your work". Outside I had a brief look at Compton MacKenzie's grave – a plain stone cross.

Beyond the cemetery was a dense carpet of short grass. I found the track marked on the 1881 map easily and followed it along an obvious terrace. Power lines also took this route. A buzzard flew just ahead. At the top Tràigh Mhór came into view. The path lead down the slope to a stone sticking out of the ground and thence to the school on the side of the road around Tràigh Mhór. I was walking along another track constructed for school children. Beyond the school the track continued to the edge of the low dune before the shore.

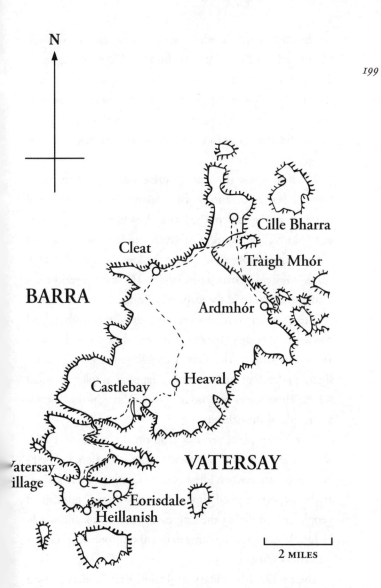

Figure 11   Barra and Vatersay

The cockle shell beach is one side of a narrow isthmus. On the other side the Atlantic breakers were coming in on Tràigh Eais. One hit a rock and spouted water high into the air. The view of Barrà to the south was dominated by the hills at the centre of the island, Heaval and Hartaval. Beinn BireabhaI was in the foreground. The sun made the sea glisten.

I walked across the school's drive and crossed the road. I had to hop a fence to continue along the gentle curve of the track to the edge of the beach. Bits of asphalt appeared in the grass. The blank blue/green windows of the airport control tower looked out across the lower dunes of Tràigh Mhór. Oyster catchers piped loudly. The dunes overlooking Tràigh Eais dwarfed the airport building.

The incoming tide had left a narrow sliver of silver sand bordered by a ring of broken pink and white shells. I walked along this strip to the airport building, crunching cockle shells under foot and watching lapping ripples of small waves. These waves bore no relation to those hitting the Atlantic side of the isthmus.

Barra's two plane services land on the sands of Tràigh Mhór at low tide creating a local tourist attraction. I remember one occasion when I flew back to Glasgow. I had arrived at the airport in good time. Gradually a large number of people arrived giving the impression that the plane would be full. When the time came to board only one other person walked forward.

The southern boundary of Tràigh Eais is marked by a low hill beyond which is a wild rocky area stretching to Cleat. The old maps show a route across this area. There is a style next to Suidheachan the house built by Compton MacKenzie on the Tràigh Eais side of the isthmus.

MacKenzie (1883–1972) first visited Barra in 1929 en

route to Eriskay to see the spot where Bonnie Prince Charlie first landed in Scotland. According to MacKenzie's biographer, Andro Linklater, he saw Barra set apart from the rest of the Highlands by "a ring of Gold". In 1934 he built the house at Suidheachan "the sitting down place ... built where one of the MacNeils of Barra used to take a rest while shooting." After MacKenzie left the island the house was converted into a factory making fertiliser from the shells of Tràigh Mhòr. Recently it was bought by a relative of MacKenzie and restored as a private residence.

I made my way through a gap between the headland and the craggy side of Beinn Bhaslain. This took me past cultivated lazy beds growing potatoes. I breasted the ridge and made my way round a massive reed bed in the dip. In a cleft between rocks a primrose bloomed.

I came to a gate hanging off its hinges but held in place by rope. There was no obvious path beyond. I continued down to the sea and made my way around the headland on the edge of the rocky foreshore. A long hessian rope was among the flotsam. This beach was devoid of sand which exposed the natural art of the rocks. There were swirls and lines, some brown, but mostly white against grey. A solitary metal fence post was stuck in a large rock right at the edge of the waves. I climbed higher to a ledge. With the eye of faith I could pick out a line of boulders marking what I thought was the old route. A rough boulder boundary also went down to the low rock cliff. There was a gap in the boundary to let the way through. I turned across the head of the valley and walked through this wild area of bare rock.

Hills to the south cupped the area. Lines of white foam stretched off across the deep sea. Burns from these hills crossed the area creating a series of deep but narrow valleys which I had to cross. Two dived into gorges before going into the sea. I had to choose my crossing point carefully but found stones configured as stepping stones. Further inland I saw a sort of ladder, an old metal style for crossing a long since vanished fence.

Once across the stream I saw a small promontory just above the sea topped by a pile of rocks. I took this to be Dun Chliobh (Dun Chilf) also known as the "Fireplace of the Kettle of Fin". The 1928 Royal Commission of Ancient and Historical Monuments Inventory comments "as it stands no more than 12 feet above the high water mark on one of the wildest shores in Scotland it must often be shrouded in spray from the Atlantic." Ahead was a grassy area rising to a point where there seemed to be broken rocks on the ground. I wondered if this was a ruined beehive house. Another ruin, maybe a chambered cairn, stood on a hill below the steep cliff forming the seaward extent of Beinn Chlaid.

The rocky cliffs which fronted Beinn Chlaid appeared to drop sheer into the sea blocking my way to Cleit. As I picked my way over the terrain I thought I might have to climb the ridge. Loose rocks on the surrounding ground made the way difficult. I had to walk inland to avoid a gorge.

Ahead the waves splashed the base of the beautiful black grey cliff. I began to climb the ridge but had not gone far before I saw a track going right under the cliff. I traced its course from the east. It seemed to pass the ruins in the direction from which I had come.

I scrambled down the slope and took the track across a shallow ford. It went down to the base of the cliff between parallel lines of boulders. Contrary to distant appearance the cliff did not fall sheer into the sea. A narrow ledge carried the track. The way was rocky but clearly discernible between the two lines of boulders. Below the track the sea was spectacular, boiling and crashing. Above the cliffs were equally spectacular. I negotiated a large boulder which had obviously been dislodged from the cliff. Then I passed another low wall with a huge boulder just opposite it. The track continued around the top of the gullies passing boulders and went through a gap in a ridge. This looked like a boundary wall. It rose along the ridge passed the cliff as a pebble based track. Here the track had been badly eroded by, I guess, rainwater from storms.

Soon the beach at Cleat came into view. The track left the rocky area and followed the top of the cliff. It became a single furrow indented in the grass, squeezed through two spurs of rock and took me to a pebble based track above Cleat beach. The track appeared to end at a burn. I walked diagonally across the beach to the back of the rocky headland, Greian Head to the west of Cleat. I passed a couple of caravans in the dunes on the west side of the beach. There was a good view of the cliffs, of Tràigh Eais and the Eoligarry headland from the beach. South Uist was also visible.

I joined the road and passed the last house in Cleat village and its semi-circular stone wall and continued along the track to the side of the hill Cnoc an Fhithich on Greian Head. I could see a track coming down from the radio mast on Cnoc an Fhithich through Barra's golf course. I turned south west and followed the fence running between the moor and the crofts, using sheep tracks where they appeared, until I got to the golf course. Like all Hebridean golf courses it is charmingly ad hoc. Grazing sheep and cattle add to the hazards and perhaps, therefore, make it more exciting to play. Two couples were playing. The 'club house' was a small larch lap shed with picture windows. All the greens were fenced to keep the animals off. The red flags marking the holes fluttered in the wind.

A pebble based track came down the hill from the radio mast. I turned downhill on this track. This gave me spectacular views over Barra's western coast south to Halaman Bay and Ben Tangaval. Ben Tangaval juts into the Atlantic cutting off the view south.

After a cattle grid the track became an asphalt road between fenced fields. I passed an old threshing machine with metal wheels. At a bend I found a gate to a path I thought went to the cemetery but the way was cut by a deep sea inlet into which a wide stream flowed in a deep channel. There was no bridge so I made do with a metal pipe which crossed the stream. The path to the cemetery had been used by the utility company which had installed the pipe. A red crate at the road side provided a style.

In 2002 the Southern Isles Amenity Trust had employed a local man, Jonathan Grant as a Countryside Ranger in Barra. He had mapped out an excellent walk from the Cemetery to Dun Bharpa, above the thatched cottage museum. This route was ideal for my purposes because it took me across the road and straight onto the moor.

After crossing the field by the roadside I was in an undulating area of rocky hills to the north of Ben Mhártainn. By keeping away from the slope I found my way to the eastern ridge on which sits the Dun.

The walk is guided by posts, which are a little confusing especially as some have fallen over. I passed Dun Cuer, an atmospheric circular iron age fortress excavated by the Sheffield University team lead by Keith Branigan.

I continued on through a broken undulating area past various ruins marked by numbered posts (the numbers corresponded to the notes in the walks leaflet). Many of the ruins date from the early nineteenth century when the crofters were cleared from the land prior to the island being sold by

General MacNeil because of bankruptcy.

A spur off the guided walk goes to Taigh Talamhanta, an iron age aisled farm excavated in the 1950s by Alison Young. I avoided this detour because I wanted simply to cross the ridge and continue to the centre of the island. I followed the posts south east to the Dun. Grant explains that this is not a Dun but a chambered cairn. There is sufficient still intact to give a good idea of the layout. A large amount of rock has been used in its construction. Most of its peripheral shaped stones are still standing. Its huge central stone, pointed to a 'V' has, however, fallen.

The area is criss-crossed by an elaborate ancient fields system mapped by Branigan. I kept to the east of this system as I wanted to retain the height I had gained on the Dun's spur. Along the way, another gem – a shaped recessed stone above a spring. Below is the thatched house museum, in a renovated thatched house. Inside is an interesting display of items depicting life in Barra. Whether open or closed, one can always take advantage of the bench in front of the house. It is a sunny spot giving a wonderful view of the hills in the centre of the island, notably Hartaval.

I did not descend to the museum. Instead I went across the moor towards a small chambered cairn which stands on top of the convex slope above the museum. There was a white horse at the ruin.

From here it was an easy walk to get to the lip of the pass Beul a' Bhealaich. It begins at a low cliff, the face marked with purple rusty stripes caused by a spring emitting from a fissure. In front of the cliff was a line of large squared stone blocks. They looked like the remains of a retaining wall or the wall of building which had leant against the rock. Higher up this pass Sheffield University have unearthed a prostrate stone "deliberately shaped by pecking." It may have been a coffin stone, a stone used to rest a coffin on the way across the pass.

This pass gives access to the east side of the island. As in South Harris when people moved to the east after clearances they continued to return west to bury their dead in their traditional cemeteries. From the pass there was a fine view of the Atlantic to the west beyond Craigston and Borve. Atlantic Ocean breakers were crashing on to the shore of tiny, homely, Barra. At the top I looked over the Minch to the east. For some reason I found myself thinking of Glasgow. How civilised it felt from this far distant spot. Soon, very soon now, I would find myself back in Glasgow. Many islanders have relatives in Glasgow whom they hope, "one day" will return home. I could think of many houses in the islands long since fallen derelict awaiting that return.

Hartaval looked splendid to the south. Beyond was the top of Heaval above a high pass. That was, perhaps, the last barrier before I reached my ultimate goal. Heillanish.

The last leg – Heaval to Heillanish

Fresh, at the beginning of a new day, I began my climb to the summit of Heaval. First I had to go around the western base of Hartaval. This lead to a valley enclosed to the east by Hartaval. Thatabhal's two peaks and Heaval's two peaks create an 'H' shaped feature. I was climbing up the middle of the 'H'.

It was hard going, so I took my time. It was the steepest hill I had climbed since the zig zags on the Rhenigidale path. The surface was largely grass covered but to one side at the top there was a large smooth bulbous rocky peak. From the col I walked forward to the lower slope of Heaval. I picked my way up to the ridge. Suddenly I was at the top and the whole sensational southern horizon opened. I walked along the ridge to the summit triangulation point. There below me the southern islands lay as dark shadows. I watched as the sun burst over the islands. Using binoculars I could pick out the lighthouse on the cliffs of Barra Head. To the east of Heaval lay the villages of Brevig and Lenish. Over the sea Skye, Coll and Tiree, Jura were all visible. I picked out the dark shape of a submarine travelling south on the surface of the Minch.

Castlebay in the sun looked delicate compared to the moors and hills which surround it. Kisimul Castle on its island and the lifeboat in the bay set off the picture. The ferry was arriving which always adds to the splendour of the scene. I spent a long time taking in the sensational view. The realisation that my goal, Vatersay the southern most inhabited island of the Outer Hebrides, was in sight took my breath away.

With mixed feelings I made my way down the west side of the summit past the cliff which forms the summit's southern face. In it is the statue is of Our Lady, Mary holding baby Jesus who in turn holds a five point star. It was carved at Pietrafana in 1954 from a bright white stone Gifford says it is about 7.3 m high but it only came up to my shoulder. In other words it is less that 2 m high.

The walk to the road was precipitous but I managed it by zig zagging between the rocks. I was back on the circular road, the A888, but I was soon off it again as I walked along the old track to Glen. This is a grassy pebble based track incised with wheel ruts. It ascended a low hill and then dropped to Glen past the gate of the local authority dump. This is well landscaped behind a dense clump of roses of a sort I have seen only in the islands. In season it bears a simple pink or dark red flower. I smiled at the realisation that my route had taken me past three local authority dumps!

The houses of Glen are a mix of gaily painted homes, greens and browns. In season there is a strong chance of flowers in gardens and around the stream. The weather on Barra seems mild compared to the more northerly islands. I passed a purple painted mobile home. I came to a junction but kept on towards the town. Kisimul Castle came into view. I passed an old style house, with a blue door, walls of cream painted corrugated iron and stone gable ends. The tower of the church came into view before the road bent above the wooden building used by a cycle hire business. It re-rejoined the A888 adjacent to the Craigard Hotel and the church.

I went into the church. The interior was remarkably plain for a Catholic church. It was wood panelled with pastel coloured washed walls. The sills of the stained glass windows each had its own pot plant. The calm atmosphere was broken only by a ticking clock. I noticed that the church had an organ and hymnals were scattered on the pews. I said a prayer of thanks for the joy I felt at reaching Castlebay.

After leaving the church I walked resolutely through Castlebay past its busy shopping street which runs down to the pier, its new community centre, its health centre and Council offices. I would have liked to visit Kisimul Castle but resolved to do that later. It is well worth a visit. Inside its high exterior walls the buildings resemble a medieval village. The Castle dates back to eleventh or twelfth centuries and is mentioned by Dean Monroe.

I walked past the Castlebay Hotel a favourite watering hole of mine, past the Co-op store, past the fascinating Heritage Centre and the School with its swimming pool open to the public in the evening. The end of my walk was in sight and I wanted to reach it.

The road to the Vatersay causeway took me past a moving and dramatic war memorial over-looking Castlebay and Vatersay. The memorial, erected in 1993, was designed by Dugald Cameron. It is a black marble pillar topped with three flying birds on a mound surrounded by a semi-circular seat. The names of those who lost their lives in both world wars have been carved in the pillar in Gaelic and English.

The road built to reach the Vatersay causeway wound up and over the hill. It had a fair width of verge but no footway. Just before the Causeway it passed a quarry which provided the rock to build the Causeway.

Vatersay

On the Vatersay side of the short causeway the road divided. Vehicles have to turn right but another road goes east past some council houses. After a short distance this modern road gives way to a pebble track which goes round Ben Orasay before rejoining the road. I turned east through a single width iron gate and found a well made pebble path bordered in places by rocks. A large fishing boat, the *Boy David*, was beached. Nearby was a decaying rowing boat. A heron flew off towards Orasay island disturbing a curlew which piped as it flew away. The path was at sea level and gave a view directly along the sound between Barra and Vatersay looking past the buoys and lights which guide shipping into Castlebay to the Cuillins across the Minch on Skye. The Hebridean sea breeze brushed my face.

On the map the island of Vatersay looks like a piece of plasticine squeezed in the middle. The hills Heishival Mór and Heishaval Beag (big and small respectively) dominate the northern bulge. Vatersay township stands on the lower lying but undulating southern bulge. The hills Ben Rulibreck and Am Meall sit at either side of the lower bulge. Heillanish, my goal, lays on the southern shore closer to the westerly headland formed by a spur from Ben Rulibreck.

I rejoined the road which ran around Cornaig Bay along a narrow ledge perched just above the water on the side of hills of Heishival Mòr and Heishival Beag. It then turned south over the shoulder of Heishival Beag and went along the northern shore of Vatersay Bay. Beyond the shoulder is a low peninsula, Uidh, which is directly across the bay from Castlebay. After going over the shoulder of Heishival Beag I passed the remains of a crashed plane lying amidst the rocks of the foreshore. This was a Catalina flying boat which crashed into the hillside in 1944. It was broken up by the RAF and brought down to the shore. The road leads to a narrow isthmus which connects the northern 'bulge' of Vatersay to the southern 'bulge'. Vatersay township is at its southern end.

The old school at the northern end of the isthmus has been renovated as a Guest House and a community hall has been built nearby. I could see cattle on the beach just north of the township. Half way down, in the western dunes, there is a memorial to those who lost their lives in a nineteenth century shipwreck. The *Lady Jane* went down in heavy seas with great loss of life whilst taking Scottish emigrants to America.

I walked through Vatersay township. It looked spruce and gay. The ruins of Vatersay House, which stand to the south west, looked gaunt by contrast but almost merged into the side of the hill. I was curious about the deserted township of Eorisdale which stands on the eastern side of the lower bulge of Vatersay, under the slopes of Am Meall. By direct line I was within a mile of Heillanish but could not resist the detour. Now I was so close to my goal I wanted the walk to go on longer.

Immediately beyond Vatersay township are high dunes

covered in grass, another grassed desert. One of the dunes has an arc of sand open in its side, like the bunker on a giant's golf course. I could see two tall old posts prominent on top of the dune but could not believe they were markers. There was no track through this green desert but there were no fences either. I walked around the lower slope of the hill Beinn Chuidher and climbed to the highest summit (68 m). This gave me a final view back over Castlebay to Heaval. But I also got an excellent view of the southern horizon, the islands to the south and my first view of Eorisdale. One house looked intact but a couple of others were reduced to their gable ends. Beyond Eorisdale there was a beautiful view out to sea across a black spit of rock. From Beinn Chuidher I walked across the soggy sward to the village.

At Eorisdale I got a strong sense of continuity with the quixotic nature of destiny. This was place where people had lived their lives, but now those lives were just memories even if some of the people themselves survived elsewhere. Thank goodness the Scottish Parliament had at long last passed the Land Reform Act in 2003. I hope that it proves a sound foundation for settling the land question once and for all.

From Eorisdale at last I turned west and climbed the headland. Now all I could see were the southern, uninhabited, Hebridean islands large and small, Sandray, Flodday, Mingulay and Berneray. I walked along the sands of the bay Bàgh á Deas. The sea was blue, the sand clean yellow. To add to the magic it was a wonderful sunny day with a clear sky. A couple of grebes swam by looking majestic. Cattle grazed on the dunes above the bay.

Heillanish came into view on the lower slopes of Ben Rulibreck. The languor of the sea lapping the shore in the bay mirrored my mood. I felt tranquil even though my heart was singing. How different this spot is to the Butt of

Lewis. The harsh ferocity of nature so dominant at the Butt had given way to the gentler side of the islands. This is why I wanted to walk from north to south, to walk from harshness, clash and clamour, to softness, harmony and tranquillity. My mood of fear and apprehension at the Butt had been replaced by peaceful joy.

A brown rock formed the low cliff. It looks as if it had boiled over the side of a black rock. A cormorant alighted in the bay. There was a little splash of heather as I crossed some rocks cupping a small sandy bay. An old creel lay on the beach wrapped round with blue rope. A snipe flew by. And then, I breasted a green hill. There were the final rocks. A curlew flew overhead, a couple of gulls wheeled above and a cormorant flew past. The grass gave way to slabs of rock which levelled down perhaps twenty or thirty feet to the sea.

There is nothing definitive to mark Heillanish. It is simply a headland of brown and black rock. A huge slab of rock pointed skyward forming a grey triangle. Perhaps that is its mark. The other rocky headland to the west is obviously not jutting so far south. A flight of ten gannets flew by close to the surface of the water.

To be absolutely sure that I had reached the end I walked out over the rocks which sloped gently to the sea. The rocks were strewn with fragments of shells, no doubt broken open by birds. I picked up a few as mementos. Then the sea came in and lapped my boots. It was an emotional moment. I had reached the southern-most point in the Hebrides.

The Outer Hebrides Way

I had a final evening in Barra waiting for the night boat back to Oban. I spent it celebrating quietly with a good meal and a beer in the Castlebay Hotel. Barra strikes me

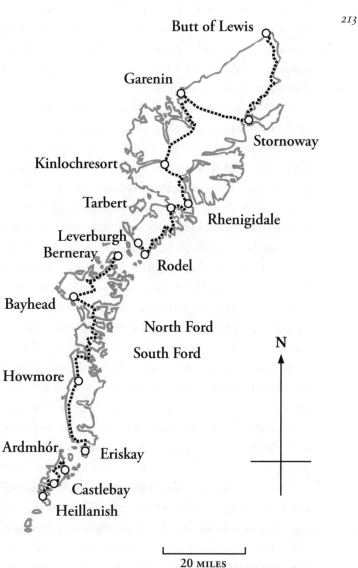

Figure 12   The Outer Hebrides Way

as a place concerned about the future but not on the edge. Visionaries like George MacLeod, the owner of the Castlebay Hotel, link the island with the outside world and have shaped its future. Barra has a reputation as a free and easy place. Barra folk, like all Hebrideans, have always preserved their independence and dignity.

The Butt of Lewis seemed a long way away: 230 miles by the route I had used. My goal had been achieved. I had walked through the islands. I had done more that just visit the places. I had done my best to be at one with the places, to understand them but leave them undisturbed.

My walk had proved that it was possible to walk from the Butt of Lewis to Heillanish using old tracks and ways. Over 50% had been off the road. I had had to jump very few fences. The way is open for others to use. The existence of historic navigational markers, standing stones, posts, lines of stones on the fords and cairns will guide today's walkers just as they have always guided walkers, in the timeless way.

Walking in this timeless way allows people to explore the whole beauty of the island chain, to gain insight into the historic context of island life and to understand better contemporary Hebridean society. This is the window in time, the timeless way, a window on the past, a light on the present.

Island roads have improved the speed and frequency of communication, reducing the risk from tides, swollen rivers and extreme weather but they have thankfully by-passed the timeless way. The route is, of course, not without risks. Crossing the tidal fords and the moors were among the most exciting parts of the walk but must be treated with the respect, the caution, they deserve. The Hebridean moors are among the last remaining wildernesses in Great Britain.

The walker must plan their day mindful of the risks and ensure they are properly equipped. The walker must always respect the wishes of the crofters and leave untouched the abundant wild life.

As it is possible to walk through the islands by this way, it is possible to design the route as a Statutory Long Distance Route. Designation will bring the route to people's attention, will secure its future, including its historic markers and encourage people to visit the islands. A wider understanding of the islands within the United Kingdom is important to us all.

My aim is to open eyes, visitors' and local eyes, to the possibilities. This is the best way of ensuring the preservation of the islands' unique environment and historic artefacts. This is far better than the slow decline and steady decay of neglect through lack of understanding or attention, or preserving the islands for the privileged few, be they lairds or nature lovers. Statutory Designation guarantees the maintenance of all these checks and balances. It will also protect the interests of the crofters.

At 230 miles the route is longer than the Southern Upland Way and over twice the length of the West Highland Way and the Offa's Dyke Path on the Welsh border. But it is shorter than the Pennine Way. It will be a challenge to those who enjoy long distance walking. The growing popularity of the Western Isles Challenge, a multi-sport team endurance race from Barra to Lewis which takes place over several days in May, supports this view. I know many who love the outdoors who regard the Outer Hebrides as their ultimate goal. I just hope that walkers who rise to this challenge will give themselves chance to become imbued with the spirit of the islands. There are places here where time can be made to stand still.

As I boarded the boat to Oban I refused to look back. But as the boat crossed the Castle Bay to enter the Minch I could not stop myself going to the back of the boat. The western horizon was still light but the lights of Castlebay twinkled in the dark, deep blue, night.

Until the next time. There will always be a next time.